Vancouver and Victoria Islands Travel

Tourism Environment

Author
Dickson Grant.

Copyright Notice

Copyright © 2017 Global Print Digital
All Rights Reserved

Digital Management Copyright Notice. This Title is not in public domain, it is copyrighted to the original author, and being published by **Global Print Digital**. No other means of reproducing this title is accepted, and none of its content is editable, neither right to commercialize it is accepted, except with the consent of the author or authorized distributor. You must purchase this Title from a vendor who's right is given to sell it, other sources of purchase are not accepted, and accountable for an action against. We are happy that you understood, and being guided by these terms as you proceed. Thank you

First Printing: 2017.

ISBN: 978-1-912483-22-8

Publisher: Global Print Digital.
Arlington Row, Bibury, Cirencester GL7 5ND
Gloucester
United Kingdom.
Website: www.homeworkoffer.com

Table of Content

Touristic Introduction 1
About Vancouver Island 4
   Indigenous People 5
   Exploration 6
   Settlement and Development 7
   Economy 9
   Population 9
History of Victoria and Vancouver Island 11
Haida Gwaii 20
   History 21
   Natural and Cultural Treasures 22
Travel and Tourism 24
   Things to Do & See 24
      Butchart Gardens 24
      Chinatown Victoria 27
      Craigdarroch Castle 28
      Emily Carr House 30
      Fisgard Lighthouse 33
      Fisherman's Wharf Victoria 35
      Fort Rodd Hill 37
      Government House 39
      Haig-Brown House 45
      Hatley Park National Historic Site 47
      Helmcken House 49
      Point Ellice House 50
      Royal British Columbia Museum 52
      Empress Hotel 55
      Craigflower Manor 59
      MacMillan Provincial Park 62
      Quw'utsun' Cultural & Conference Centre 64
   Attractions 67
      Beaches 67
      Festivals & Events on Vancouver Island 86
      Hot Springs 91
      Kid's Stuff on Vancouver Island and BC Gulf Islands 93
      Llama Walks and Llama Hiking 99
      Maritime Museum of British Columbia 106

Royal British Columbia Museum 115
  Petroglyphs 117
  Totem Poles around Vancouver Island 123
  Wineries 127
  Fishing & Guides 131
  Golf & Golf Vacations 133
  Kayaking & Canoeing Adventures 135
  Whale Watching 136
Nearby Regions & Towns *137*
  Parksville 137
  Port Alberni 152
  Coombs 167
  Errington 174
Transportation *180*
Calendar of Events Vancouver Island *183*

Touristic Introduction

Vancouver Island, BC, 31 285 km2, the largest island on the West Coast of North America, is about 460 km long and 50-120 km wide and stretches parallel to the British Columbia mainland. It is separated from the mainland by the Georgia, Queen Charlotte and Johnstone straits and from the United States by Juan de Fuca Strait.

Tourism on Vancouver Island is far more than an impressive set of facts and figures. Yes, it's true the sector generates a whopping $2.2 billion annually for the Island's economy, making tourism either first or second on the list of economic drivers in every community in the region. Statistics also show that tourism accounts for more than 60,000 Island jobs and that its revenues have increased nearly 50 percent since the turn of the century.

Beyond this, however, tourism is deeply embedded in the very fabric of life on this genuinely super, natural slice of West Coast paradise. For one thing, it's a source of no small amount of pride to residents that their Island home is repeatedly named one of the top travel destinations in the world by Canadian and international travel journalists, editors and the readers of such A-list publications as *Condé Nast Traveler, Islands* and *Travel + Leisure*. All this glowing media coverage, in fact, is worth approximately $4 million annually in advertising equivalency.

On a bricks and mortar level, the Island's radiantly healthy tourism sector is responsible for many of the amenities and experiences that local families and residents enjoy in their respective communities

ourism has a direct impact on the development of restaurants, resorts, B&Bs, galleries, mountain bike facilities, elements parks and golf courses. It fuels revenues in the retail and transportation sectors, and contributes to audience numbers for concerts, theatre productions and a wide range of festivals. And there's no question that along with their pocketbooks, off-island visitors and staycationing residents bring enthusiasm and excitement to Island communities while also helping locals appreciate their own backyards with fresh wonder.

Victoria Island

Geology
Victoria Island is largely composed of sedimentary rock. There is a belt of Precambrian rock on the west coast and another on the south

coast, veined with copper formerly used by the COPPER INUIT. The northwestern part of the island is mainly composed of the Shaler Mountains, which reach above 600 m. The island's largest river, Kuujjua (Inuktitut, "big river"), rises in the mountains and flows into Minto Inlet. The east side is a flat lowland that rises to prominent cliffs on the Wollaston Peninsula. The glacial landforms are more complex than those on any of the other arctic islands. The rivers of the lowlands follow gently wandering courses and there are numerous lakes. The rock formations as well as the shape of the south coast closely resemble those of CORONATION GULF immediately to the south.

About Vancouver Island

Description

With the Haida Gwaii, Vancouver Island forms part of a partially submerged chain of the Western Cordillera and is a continuation of the US coastal mountains. Its coastline is very rugged, especially on the west, where there are several fjordlike inlets - the longest being Alberni Inlet and Muchalat Inlet - that cut into a heavily forested, mountainous interior. The highest peaks are Golden Hinde (2200 m), Elkhorn Mountain (2195 m) and Mount Colonel Foster (2135 m) within Strathcona Provincial Park, and Victoria Peak (2163 m), which lies north of the park.

In contrast to this mountainous core are the coastal lowlands, which form an almost encircling belt. They are most pronounced in the north and east where the Nahwitti and Nanaimo lowlands form part of a coastal trough stretching from southeastern Alaska to the Puget Depression in Washington state.

Vancouver Island has numerous freshwater lakes, the largest being Nimpkish, Cowichan, Buttle, Sproat, Great Central and Campbell. There are no dominant river systems on the Island, although numerous rivers open up to the coast through broad valleys and terminate in extensive delta and estuary complexes. These include the Nimpkish, Campbell, Somass, Salmon, Gold, Nanaimo, Nitnat and Cowichan rivers. Many of the Island's numerous other rivers and creeks are characterized by steep and narrow valleys, reflecting the rugged topography, particularly on the west coast.

The climate of Vancouver Island is damp but mild, with precipitation ranging over 3 m in the western flanks of the mountains to less than 0.8 m in the southeastern Nanaimo Lowland. Much of the precipitation is received in the winter and returns to the Pacific through a series of rapid-flowing, deeply incised, relatively short rivers such as the Nanaimo and Campbell.

Indigenous People

Although the archaeological record is still incomplete, it is clear that Indigenous people have occupied Vancouver Island for several thousand years. A tribal village society evolved with an economy based on fishing, collecting and hunting. The abundant marine and forest resources along the coasts supported a culture rich in oral tradition and artistic expression. Two main linguistic families, Salishan and Wakashan, developed and continue to exist.

Traditionally, villages comprised stoutly constructed cedar longhouses and were usually situated in sheltered coves or a short distance upriver from the ocean. During the hunting season bands migrated through well-defined territories. In the early 19th century the Indigenous population was about 15 000. Owing to disease, it declined to about 5600 in 1881, remained around 5000 until the 1950s, but increased to more than 7000 by the 1970s. The number is now double of what it was the 19th century, or 5% of the Island's population. (See also Ditidaht, Nuu-chah-nulth, Pacheenaht, Ahousaht, Chickliset, Ehattesaht, Hesquiaht, Mowachaht, Muchalaht, Nutchatlaht, Opetchesaht, Sheshaht, Tla-o-qui-aht, Toquaht, Uchucklesaht, Ucluelet).

Exploration

Spanish, Russian, French, British and American explorers and traders began penetrating the waters of the northeastern Pacific in the 18th century. Britain gradually ousted the others, however, through the activities of its trading companies, the Royal Navy's presence and negotiation and threat in Europe. The voyage of James Cook and George Vancouver's circumnavigation and hydrographic survey of Vancouver Island (1792-94) provided the basis for increased British penetration. The diversity of place names with which the Island and its surrounding islands and waters abound are a permanent record of this exploratory period.

Settlement and Development

In 1843 the Hudson's Bay Company sent James Douglas to Vancouver Island to select a site for a fort, and a small settlement at the southern tip developed around Fort Victoria. The Treaty of Washington established the Island as British territory; it was made a British crown colony in 1849. Vancouver Island united with the mainland BC colony in 1866, and the united colony entered the Dominion of Canada as the province of British Columbia in 1871.

The European population grew slowly until the late 1850s, when the discovery of gold on the mainland (see Fraser River Gold Rush; Cariboo Gold Rush) and coal on the Island led to a significant increase. Some of those disappointed in the gold fields turned to farming and coal mining and joined a growing trickle of settlers carving out homesteads on the narrow eastern lowlands.

Besides Victoria, early settlement centered on the Duncan area of the Cowichan River valley and the Courtenay-Comox region, both attractive and fertile valleys. Although the forest was an obstacle to the pioneer farmer, its vast size and the high quality of its trees stimulated the growth of lumber mills at points accessible to tidewater, such as Port Alberni (1861) and Chemainus (1862). The Esquimalt and Nanaimo Railway (1886) provided the basis for expanding the Island's lumber and mining industries. By 1900 the population had grown to around 51 000, with nearly 90% concentrated in the Victoria-Nanaimo region.

After 1900 the pace of development increased rapidly as immigration continued and the mining and lumbering industries developed. Nanaimo expanded and new coal mines were opened at Cumberland, Ladysmith and Union Bay. Population growth slowed between 1921 and 1941, as little suitable land for agricultural development remained; the exhaustion of the best coal deposits left further development to the expansion of the forest industry. The potential for tourism was also becoming apparent as transportation facilities improved and as the attraction of the Island as a retirement area grew.

Economy

The evolution of Vancouver Island's economy has been strongly tied to its rich endowment of natural resources. This endowment has helped create a solid economic base leading to the development of healthy communities and a well-developed social and economic infrastructure throughout all areas of the Island.

As with any resource-dependent economy, Vancouver Island has suffered the effects of "boom or bust" economic cycles. Since the 1980s, however, the Island has experienced change that extends beyond the cyclical swings of the international economy. Indeed, many industries such as the forest industry have made permanent structural changes in order to remain competitive in the global marketplace. At the same time, many new industries and businesses have been attracted to Vancouver Island by its outstanding "quality of life" features. Examples include high-technology firms, recreation and tourism and small manufacturing.

Population

Communities on Vancouver Island also show a remarkable degree of variation. In the northern and western areas of the Island, they rely heavily on the forest sector as a source of income. During recent years, with low world prices for forest products, particularly pulp, and downsizing of the industry, these communities have experienced considerable hardship. This has resulted in higher levels of unemployment and social assistance and, in some cases, population declines as people have chosen to move away.

By contrast, communities on the southern and eastern portions of Vancouver Island are highly diversified and are experiencing vigorous population increases, which in turn is fuelling economic growth. The population of the Island was 495 000 in 1981 and 663 000 in 2001, an increase of 34%. Much of the growth occurred in the Capital and Nanaimo regional districts. Most of the population on the Island lives in urban areas (nearly 80%). In many instances this growth represents its own problems, such as traffic congestion, soaring property and housing prices and urban and rural sprawl. These and other problems challenge the Island's otherwise attractive quality of life and have lead to much discussion and conflict, including the debate surrounding the Vancouver Island Land Use Plan prepared by BC's Commission on Resources and Environment (1994).

History of Victoria and Vancouver Island

Captain James Cook, R.N. 1778

In the spring of 1778 Captain James Cook, R.N., became the first known European to set foot on what is now British Columbia. Permanent European settlement, long delayed, was brought about by the gradual overland penetration of the fur trade companies towards the Pacific Coast. On March 13, 1843, Chief Factor of the Hudson's Bay Company James Douglas, accompanied by the pioneer Roman Catholic missionary Father J.B.Z. Bolduc, anchored off Clover Point in the "Beaver." The next day he selected the site for Fort Victoria. By mid-June Chief Factor Charles Ross was busy at work constructing the new post.

The Hudson's Bay Company - 1843

Hence the City of Victoria was founded by the Hudson's Bay Company on March 14, 1843, as a trading post and fort at the location the native Indians called "Camosack" meaning "place where Camass is gathered" and refers to the land stretching from Victoria harbour to Gonzales point, which Chief Factor James Douglas found relatively clear and ready for farming when he arrived to survey possible fort sites in 1843. The Songhees women cultivated this area to ensure a plentiful supply of Camass lily, of which the bulb was gathered and dried to make cakes and other foods for winter. Esquimalt, originally pronounced "Is-whoy-malth" means "place of shoaling waters". Anticipating that under the Oregon Treaty, then being drawn up, the 49th parallel would be chosen as the International Boundary Line, the Hudson's Bay Company moved its fort from Vancouver on the Columbia River to the southern end of Vancouver Island. Thereafter, for a short time, it was known locally as "Fort Albert," but by resolution passed by the Council of the Northern Department of the Company meeting at Fort Garry on June 10, 1843, it was officially named "Fort Victoria" after the great British Queen.

To buttress the British claim north of the 49th parallel, the Hudson's Bay Company, by Royal Grant dated January 13, 1849, received title to the whole of Vancouver Island, but only on condition that colonization should be undertaken. By midsummer Chief Factor James Douglas was in residence at Fort Victoria to begin this task, with the assistance of his colleagues in the fur trade.

Crown Colony of Vancouver Island - 1849

Constitutional history began in 1849 with the creation by the Imperial Government of the Crown Colony of Vancouver Island and on March 11, 1850, Richard Blanshard formally assumed office as Governor of the Colony of Vancouver Island. It was a wintry day, but every effort was made to make the ceremony as impressive as the rudeness of the surroundings at Fort Victoria would permit. A salute of seventeen guns roared out from "H.M.S. Driver" and was answered from the bastion of the fort. All available British residents and a complement of sailors from the "Driver" were assembled in front of the fort to hear the newly-arrived Governor read the Royal Commission, appointing him the first Governor of the first Crown Colony to be established in British territory west of the Great Lakes.

City Incorporation - 1862

The name "Victoria" was adopted when the town site was laid out in 1852. Victoria was incorporated as a City on August 2, 1862. Mr. Thomas Harris was elected (by acclamation) as Victoria's first Mayor on August 16, 1862, and he presided at the City Council's first meeting held on August 25, 1862.

The Gold Rush - 1858

The life of the little community of Victoria, numbering 450 men, women and children in 1853, centered in the business of the Hudson's Bay Company until 1858 when gold was discovered on the mainland of British Columbia. Then miners and adventurers from the gold fields of California and Australia, and indeed from all parts of the world, flocked to Victoria which was the only ocean port and outfitting centre for the gold fields of the Caribou.

The first ship bringing these modern argonauts, the "Commodore" - a wooden side-wheel American steamer, entered Victoria harbour on Sunday morning, April 25, 1858, just as the townspeople were returning homeward from church. With astonishment, they watched as 450 men disembarked - typical gold-seekers, complete with blankets, miner's pans and spades and firearms; and it is estimated that within a few weeks, over 20,000 had landed.

The gold rush was on in earnest and the quiet of Victoria shattered forever. Overnight, as it were, a City of tents sprang up around the fort and quickly spread out over both sides of James Bay. While the great majority of these people were only transients, the rush of gold-seekers on the way to the diggings on the Fraser River suddenly transformed "Fort Victoria" from a sleepy village into a bustling commercial centre.

A wild land-boom followed, and one reads of city lots that were going begging one day at $25 apiece, being eagerly snapped up a week later at $3,000 each.

With the discovery of gold on the Fraser and Thompson Rivers on the mainland, and in consequence of the ensuing "rush," the Crown Colony of British Columbia was inaugurated at Fort Langley on November 19, 1858, with the subsequent decision to "lay out and settle the site of a city to be the capital of British Columbia on February 14, 1859, at New Westminster."

Union of the Colonies - 1866

With the waning of the gold excitement, the continued separate existence of the Crown Colonies of Vancouver Island and British Columbia became costly and impractical. Early in August 1866, an Act for the Union of the colonies was passed by the Imperial Parliament. It became effective at noon on November 19, 1866, when it was proclaimed simultaneously in the two capitals. In Victoria, there was no rejoicing, and in New Westminster only a "small knot of people" gathered in front of the government offices to hear the Acting High Sheriff of British Columbia, J.A.R. Homer, read the proclamation. Not a cheer was raised.

"The Birdcages"

Parliamentary government in British Columbia dates back to August 12, 1856, when Governor James Douglas convened the first Legislative Assembly of Vancouver Island within Fort Victoria. In 1859 government buildings were constructed at James Bay, south Fort, and christened "The Birdcages." In continuous use for almost forty years (except for the brief period 1866-68 when New Westminster, not Victoria, was the capital) they were replaced in the 1890's by the present Parliament Buildings, completed late in 1897. The formal opening took place on February 10, 1898, when Lieutenant Governor R.R. MacInnes drove up in his carriage to open the first session of the Provincial Legislature to be held in the new buildings.

Confederation - The Capital City - 1871

On July 21, 1871, British Columbia became the sixth province of the Dominion of Canada and Victoria was proclaimed the Capital City. The achievement of Confederation was no simple undertaking. The colonial legislative Council had for weeks in March, 1870, debated the terms of union and, agreement reached, three delegates were appointed to negotiate with the federal government. Dr. J.S. Helmcken from Victoria, Dr. R.W.W. Carrall from Cariboo, and Hon. J.W. Trutch, senior government official, left Victoria on May 10 and, traveling of necessity most of the way through the United States, reached Ottawa early in June to begin the negotiations which were to reach their culmination the following year. With Confederation, the continued establishment of the British or Canadian naval and military headquarters on the Pacific at Esquimalt, adjoining Victoria, was guaranteed.

A Brief Biography

Victoria is Western Canada's oldest city. The City began in 1843 as a Hudson Bay Company trading post, named in honour of Queen Victoria.

With the Fraser Valley gold rush in 1858, Victoria grew rapidly as the main port of entry to the Colonies of Vancouver Island and British Columbia. When the colonies combined, the City became the colonial capital and was established as the provincial capital when British Columbia joined the Canadian Confederation in 1871.

For most of the nineteenth century, Victoria remained the largest city in British Columbia and was the foremost in trade and commerce. However, with construction of the Transcontinental railway, Vancouver, as its terminus, emerged as the major west coast port and the largest city in British Columbia.

In the twentieth century, Victoria evolved primarily as a city of government, retirement and tourism. The City remains, however, Canada's western naval base and home to a major fishing fleet. Ship building and repair, as well as forest products and machine manufacturing industries, continue as significant sources of employment. Increasingly, the city is developing as a marine, forestry and agricultural research centre. The City is also noted for its fine educational institutions which include the University of Victoria, Lester B. Pearson College of the Pacific (one of only six in the world operated by United World Colleges), and the recently opened Royal Roads University.

Today with an estimated regional population of 326,000, a moderate climate and scenic setting, Victoria has retained a very vital but comfortable quality of life. The City is proud of its British heritage, its fine homes and neighbourhoods, its historic and attractive downtown, the flowers and parks and, of course, the Inner Harbour with its vistas toward the famous Empress Hotel and the Parliament Buildings.

In a survey conducted by Conde Nast Traveler magazine, Victoria was judged to be one of the world's best cities, topping the list in the category of environment and ambience. In a cross-Canada survey, Victoria residents registered the greatest satisfaction with their city. This satisfaction and regard for the quality of life and environment is perhaps the most notable feature of Victoria today, and the challenge in its future.

Victoria Today

Greater Victoria, which includes the adjoining municipalities of Saanich, Oak Bay and Esquimalt, has a population of over 330,000; it enjoys an average winter day temperature of 5.5 degrees Celsius (42 degrees Fahrenheit), summer 16.1 degrees Celsius (61 degrees Fahrenheit), and annual rainfall of only 68.5 centimeters (27 inches) and an average of six hours bright sunshine daily throughout the year. The City is sea-girt on the south and east, and on the north and west is bounded by farm lands stretching back into the great forests of Vancouver Island.

Haida Gwaii

The Haida Gwaii include about 150 islands in a scimitar-shaped archipelago 250 km long. Graham and Moresby Islands comprise the bulk of the 10 000 km2 area. Separated by 48-140 km of open water (Hecate Strait) from the mainland islands, the Haida Gwaii are among the most isolated islands in Canada.

The Haida Gwaii is a group of islands off the north coast of British Columbia. The name means "Islands of the People" in the language of the Haida, who claim the archipelago as their ancestral lands. Captain George Dixon named this group of islands the Queen Charlotte Islands in 1787 after one of his ships, which in turn was named for the wife of King George III, and this was its official name until 2010 when Haida Gwaii was accepted.

The Haida Gwaii include about 150 islands in a scimitar-shaped archipelago 250 km long. Graham and Moresby Islands comprise the bulk of the 10 000 km2 area. Separated by 48-140 km of open water

(Hecate Strait) from the mainland islands, the Haida Gwaii are among the most isolated islands in Canada. Also unique is the absence of a continental shelf off the steep western ramparts of Moresby Island.

History

Archaeological evidence indicates human occupation of the Haida Gwaii for at least 6000 to 8000 years. Juan Pérez was the first European to sight the islands (1774). They were visited by James Cook in 1778. At that time the Haida nation populated the islands and probably numbered 6000 to 8000. European diseases drastically lowered the Haida population to about 588 individuals in 1915, the most dramatic drop for any tribe recorded in the province. The present population of all peoples on Haida Gwaii is about 5000.

Until recently, most people were loggers, fishermen or miners in the villages of Masset, Port Clements (incorporated 1982), and Queen Charlotte (incorporated 2005), and the communities of Old Massett, Skidegate, Sandspit and Tlell. Today geologists, biologists and recreationists come to study and enjoy the rugged mountain scenery (peaks up to 1200 m) along the western backbone of the islands, spectacular fjords, seabird and sea lion colonies, dark giant Sitka spruce and cedar forests, and remnants of decaying Haida totem poles.

Natural and Cultural Treasures

The Haida Gwaii were formed by the movement of huge plates under the Pacific Ocean from the region of the South Pacific to their present location (see Plate Tectonics). Unlike most of Canada during the last Ice Age, parts of the Haida Gwaii escaped glaciation. This, coupled with the islands' isolation, has resulted in these islands becoming a biologically unique area in Canada. There are numerous plants here that are found either only on the Haida Gwaii or in distant lands such as Japan.

All the native land mammals and 3 kinds of birds are subspecifically unique, with the black bear being the largest in North America. Unfortunately, introduced species have been taking their toll on many native plants and animals. Several species of seabirds are now at risk because of the threats posed by introduced predators (rats, squirrels and raccoons).

The old Haida village of Ninstints (SGang Gwaay Ilnagaay), on Anthony Island (SGang Gwaay), has been made a United Nations World Heritage Site. Conservation measures to slow the natural degradation of its spectacular totem poles hope to extend their existence as part of a collection of world treasures.

The cultural and natural features of the Haida Gwaii draw tourists. Naikoon Provincial Park, with its vast beaches and bogs, attracts hikers. The South Moresby area, with its outstanding totem poles, marine life, hot springs, forests and mountain scenery, is unrivalled in Canada as a place to explore by water. In 1993 this area was protected by the creation of Gwaii Haanas National Park Reserve and in 2010, the adjacent marine waters received protection with the establishment of the Gwaii Haanas National Marine Conservation Area Reserve.

Travel and Tourism
Things to Do & See
Butchart Gardens

The Butchart Gardens, tucked into a serene 50-acre country estate on the southeast corner of Vancouver Island, is a garden of earthly delights in every season. From summer splendour to autumn's golden glory and sparkling holiday magic there's always something to see, learn and experience.

Fifty acres of floral finery offering spectacular views as you stroll along meandering paths and expansive lawns. In 1904, the concept of The Butchart Gardens began with an effort to beautify a worked-out quarry site on the 130-acre estate of Mr. and Mrs. R.P. Butchart, pioneers in the manufacture of Portland Cement in Canada. Their endeavour became a family commitment to horticulture and hospitality spanning more than 90 years and delighting visitors from all over the world. From the exquisite Sunken Garden to the charming

Rose Garden, this 50-acre show-place still maintains the gracious traditions of the past, in one of the loveliest corners in the world.

The Butchart Gardens are located in Brentwood Bay, 21 km north of the capital city of Victoria and 20 km south of the Vancouver Victoria ferry terminal at Swartz Bay.

Winter romance and tranquility:

January March

The Gardens in winter never truly sleep. Snowdrops and crocuses awaken, forming a pretty carpet of blooms. Winter flowering trees and shrubs dot the grounds as spring approaches.

Spring Colour Spectacular:

April May

Spring comes early on Vancouver Island and this season is like a breath of fresh air. Gardeners plant over 100,000 tulip bulbs and their dazzling splendour greets visitors with rivers of colour a sight to behold in the warm spring sunshine.

Summer's Simply Dazzling:

June September 15

Summer is absolutely splendid at The Gardens. Glorious blooms are at their peak and a visit at this time of year transcends the ordinary.

Autumn Cascade of Colours:

September 16 November

Autumn's golden glory is a sight to behold. You'll love The Gardens at this time of year.

Holiday spirit flourishes at Christmas

December 1- January 6

Replacing the autumn colours of November come sparkling and unique Christmas lights setting the evenings aglow from December 1 to January 6. Carollers and festive entertainment complement the atmosphere for a perfect family visit to The Butchart Gardens at Christmas Time. Holiday magic weaves a spell during "Christmas Time". By night, The Gardens are a magical sight as a lavish display of lights illuminates the sky.

May we suggest a late afternoon visit (after 3 p.m.) from June through September; enjoy the flowers by daylight, stop for refreshment and some light musical entertainment, then see the Gardens again by the romantic Night Illuminations thousands of lights in dozens of hues dramatically light the Gardens. On Saturday evenings, June 29 through August 31, the popular Saturday Fireworks shows can cause long line-ups to enter The Gardens. Please expect delays at the admissions gate if arriving after 3 p.m. on Fireworks Saturdays.

Contact Details:

Butchart Gardens

800 Benvenuto Avenue

Brentwood Bay

Victoria

BC V8M 1J8

Toll Free: 1-866-652-4422

Recorded Information: 250-652-5256

Chinatown Victoria

The splendid lion-bedecked Gate of Harmonious Interest marks the entrance to the small Chinatown in Victoria, BC, the oldest in Canada and the second oldest in North America, after Chinatown in San Francisco. The history of Chinatown goes back to the mid-nineteenth century with the mass influx of gold miners from California to what is now British Columbia in 1858.

Victoria's revitalized Chinatown remains an active place for Chinese-Canadians and is a popular destination for local residents and visitors alike. Once a ghetto for newcomers, Chinatown is now a heritage area, a vibrant commercial community, and an intriguing part of Victoria's past and present.

Some of the tourist attractions of Chinatown are the old Chinese School, the famously narrow Fan Tan Alley, and its ornate gate on Government Street at Fisgard Street, the Gate of Harmonious Interest, which was built in Suzhou in Jiangsu Province, Eastern China. Be sure to visit the tiny shops and studios on Fan Tan Alley, the narrowest street in Canada only 90 centimetres wide at its narrowest point (35 inches).

The focus of Chinatown is the 500-600 block of Fisgard Street, but many of Chinatown's most historical and important places are out of public view, like the Tam Kung Buddhist Temple, which is the oldest of its kind in Canada.

Craigdarroch Castle

Craigdarroch Castle in Victoria is an imposing Victorian mansion completed in 1890 for Robert and Joan Dunsmuir, Scottish immigrants who made their fortune from Vancouver Island coal.

Robert Dunsmuir died in 1889, just months before his majestic Craigdarroch Castle was completed. Although he arrived on Vancouver Island a poor coal miner, he built an empire and became the wealthiest and most influential man in British Columbia.

The fortune Dunsmuir amassed is reflected in every piece of the finest wood, stone and glass meticulously tooled to create Craigdarroch Castle, now a national historic museum featuring an extensive collection of stained and lead glass windows, magnificent woodwork, Victorian furnishings and decorative arts.

To tour the Castle, you can park on the Castle lot or on the street where indicated. You enter through the old coach entrance, pay your admission fee, clean your shoes and are then provided with a floor map, family history and introduction as to how to proceed. Tours are self-guided, so you can stop where you want. It should take you 45 minutes to an hour to tour through the Castle.

It is an easy climb up the 87 stairs, stopping on all of the four floors to tour the various rooms and then to the Tower for a panoramic view of Victoria, the Strait of Juan de Fuca and the snow capped Olympic Mountains. There are volunteer docents (information providers) available throughout the Castle. If you have any questions, ask someone with a badge and they will be happy to assist you.

A visit to Craigdarroch Castle is essential to truly appreciate the lavish lifestyle Joan Dunsmuir and her family enjoyed.

Opening Hours:
Open daily: 10 am 4:30 pm

Extended hours from June 15 to Labour Day: 9 am 7 pm

Closed Christmas Day (Dec 25)

Closed Boxing Day (Dec 26)

Closed New Year's Day (Jan 1)

Contact Details:

Craigdarroch Castle

1050 Joan Crescent (Off Fort Street)

Victoria, BC

V8S 3L5

Telephone: 250-592-5323

Directions:

An easy eight-minute drive from the inner harbour, up Fort Street, right on Joan Crescent. Parking is available. A 40-45 minute walk from the inner harbour, up Fort Street, along Antique Row and various interesting shops and sights.

Emily Carr House

With an architecture described as both "San Francisco Victorian" and "English Gingerbread," all agree that the heritage Emily Carr House is on the must-see list of attractions in Victoria.

Centrally located only four blocks from Victoria's Inner Harbour and the Provincial Legislature buildings, Emily Carr House offers its visitors a chance to gain an insight into Canada's first, and best known, independent artist and writer.

Emily Carr was born here in 1871, a scant six months after British Columbia moved from British colonial status to becoming a province of the world's newest nation. She used her brushes and pens to proclaim her pride in this part of Canada for the rest of her life.

Emily developed a passion for nature, animals and art, and at age seventeen studied painting first in San Francisco and later in Paris and London. After teaching art to children in Vancouver, she returned to Victoria in 1913 and built the "House of All Sorts", a boarding house for anyone who needed shelter. She undertook a series of ambitious journeys into the remote wilderness, visited isolated native villages, and drew inspiration from the hundreds of sketches and water-colours she brought back from these journeys.

Millie, as she was known to her family and friends, started writing in her later years as her health failed. In 1941 she published her novel Klee Wyck which won the Governor's General's Award. She wrote several other best sellers, including The Book of Small and The Heart of a Peacock. Emily Carr died on March 2 1945 and was buried on the Carr Family plot at the Ross Bay Cemetery in Victoria.

In the restored rooms of the house, built in 1864, you'll enter into the same Victorian ambiance the Carr family would have known in the 1870s, and upstairs are several of their actual possessions, including some of Emily's pottery and sculpture.

One room is now used as the "People's Gallery" to present the work of Canadian artists, and at the rear of the house a small gift shop offers a remarkably varied selection of items produced by Victoria artists and potters.

Emily Carr House is near the Inner Harbour of Victoria, at 207 Government Street, only a 10-minute walk south from the Royal B.C. Museum and the Legislative Buildings. The house is open to the general public from May to September; Tuesday to Saturday from 10 am to 4 pm. Admission fees are in effect. Special openings are scheduled at other times of the year, especially in December.

Contact details:
Emily Carr House
207 Government Street
Victoria, BC

V8V 2K3

Telephone: 250-383-5843

Fisgard Lighthouse

Fisgard Lighthouse in Victoria is nationally important as the first lighthouse on the rocky Pacific west coast of Canada. Built by the British when Vancouver Island was still a crown colony, Fisgard Lighthouse has stood as a symbol of sovereignty since its construction in 1860. The lighthouse is still in operation but is now fully operational.

Along with nearby Race Rocks Lighthouse in the Strait of Juan de Fuca, Fisgard still provides a welcome guide for mariners to Royal Roads anchorage and the Esquimalt naval base (CFB Esquimalt), and also points the way to Victoria harbour for merchant ships and recreational vessels.

The former keeper's house now contains exhibits, artifacts, children's games, and hands-on display panels. Panoramic views from the lighthouse include tall ships at the Canadian Naval Base, Esquimalt lagoon, and the snow-capped Olympic Mountains across the Strait of Juan de Fuca.

Access to Fisgard Lighthouse is through the large grounds of historic Fort Rodd Hill, a coast artillery fort overlooking the entrance to

Esquimalt Harbour, built in the late 1890s to protect Victoria and the Royal Naval base.

There is a pleasant walk from the Fort Rodd Hill field to the lighthouse, but rather than following the direct route, you can take the nature path, near the picnic tables, for a 10-minute stroll through a forest, with many sights and bird sounds along the way. The gravel walkway to the lighthouse was built over a torpedo net meant to intercept torpedoes fired at the naval base.

As you walk along the trails, look for some of the year-round residents who call Fort Rodd Hill home, including Colombian Black-tailed deer, grey squirrels, raccoons and numerous bird species. The waters around Fisgard Lighthouse are frequented by harbour seals and the occasional sea lion.

Fort Rodd Hill and Fisgard Lighthouse are 14 km from downtown Victoria. These two adjoining National Historic Sites can be accessed off Highway 1, take the Colwood exit or off Highway 1A, onto Ocean Boulevard in Colwood.

Please note that pets and bicycles are not allowed in the sites.

Opening Hours:

February 15 October 31: 10:00 a.m. to 5:30 p.m.

November 1 February 14: 9:00 a.m. to 4:30 p.m.

Contact Details:

603 Fort Rodd Hill Road

Colwood

Victoria, BC

V9C 2W8

Tel: 250-478-5849

Fax: 250-478-2816

Fisherman's Wharf Victoria

Just around the corner from Victoria's Inner Harbour and the Ogden Point cruise ship terminal, Fisherman's Wharf is a hidden treasure waiting to be discovered.

This unique marine destination offers food and ice cream kiosks, unique shops and eco-tour adventures in the heart of the working harbour. Wander down the docks with your lunch, buy seafood fresh off the boat, see moored pleasure vessels and float homes, and watch as working fishing vessels unload their catches.

Adventures include whale watching and wildlife-viewing tours, kayak rentals and fishing charters. Located at 1 Dallas Road in Victoria, a scenic 10-minute walk from downtown, Fisherman's Wharf is serviced by harbour ferries from one of the many Inner Harbour pick up spots.

The eastern end of Fisherman's Wharf is populated largely by colouful float homes, which serves as permanent homes to their owners, just steps from the bustling and festive commercial plaza so popular with tourists and visitors. The residents share their lively neighbourhood with harbour seals, herons, eagles, geese, cormorants, gulls, otters and raccoons.

If you can't make it down to Fisherman's Wharf, you can entertain yourself at home by watching Eagle Wing Tours' underwater live streaming Seal Cam located near their office in Fisherman's Wharf. You may see river otters, harbour seals, a variety of small fish such as perch, stickleback, herring and salmon, and jellyfish, plankton, and crab larvae.

Fisherman's Wharf was built after the Second World War to accommodate commercial fishing vessels, opening in March 1948. Located in Victoria's Middle Harbour, the original 120-metre (390 foot) wharf could moor 60 fish-packing ships along six finger float piers. More Information: www.fishermanswharfvictoria.com

Fort Rodd Hill

Fort Rodd Hill, a coast artillery fort overlooking the entrance to Esquimalt Harbour in Victoria, was built by the British in the late 1890s to protect Victoria and the Royal Naval base in Esquimalt.

From 1878 until 1956, a system of artillery positions guarded the city of Victoria and Esquimalt Harbour. Originally a link in the worldwide chain of defences for the British Empire, this system evolved into a watchdog for Canada's security and sovereignty of our Pacific west coast.

The "Victoria-Esquimalt Fortress" grew and changed over time to deal with new threats and technologies. Fort Rodd Hill represents all of the defensive locations of the Victoria-Esquimalt Fortress, and is one of the best preserved and most complete examples of its kind, consisting entirely of original structures, with minimal restoration.

Stroll along the ramparts of three coastal gun batteries built a century ago. Look down the barrels of original guns, explore underground magazines and discover camouflaged searchlight emplacements. Continue through the picturesque grounds to view the original Command posts, guardhouses and troop barracks.

There are numerous interpretive signs and audio-visual stations, as well as period-furnished rooms. As you walk along the trails, look for some of the year-round residents who call Fort Rodd Hill home, including Colombian Black-tailed deer, grey squirrels, raccoons and numerous bird species.

The large grounds also boast the Fisgard Lighthouse, the first permanent lighthouse on Canada's west coast, which has been in continuous use since 1860.

There is a pleasant walk from the field to the lighthouse, but rather than following the direct route, you can take the nature path, near the picnic tables, for a 10-minute stroll through a forest, with many sights and bird sounds along the way. The gravel walkway to the lighthouse was built over a torpedo net meant to intercept torpedoes fired at the naval base.

The former keeper's house now contains exhibits, artifacts and display panels. The waters around Fisgard Lighthouse are frequented by harbour seals and the occasional sea lion.

A Parks Canada initiative allows visitors the opportunity to stay overnight at Fort Rodd Hill, in sturdy tent cabins. Amenities include kitchen facilities, barbecues, picnic tables and bathrooms. After the grounds close, campers have the whole site to ourselves and are free to further explore the grounds. A Reservation through Parks Canada is required to stay overnight at Fort Rodd Hill.

Fort Rodd Hill and Fisgard Lighthouse are 14 km from downtown Victoria. These two adjoining National Historic Sites can be accessed off Highway 1, by taking the Colwood exit, or off Highway 1A, onto Ocean Boulevard in Colwood.

Please note that pets and bicycles are not allowed in the sites.

Opening Hours:

February 15 October 31: 10:00 a.m. to 5:30 p.m.

November 1 February 14: 9:00 a.m. to 4:30 p.m.

Contact Details:

603 Fort Rodd Hill Road

Colwood

Victoria, BC

V9C 2W8

Tel: 250-478-5849

Fax: 250-478-2816

Government House

Government House is the office and official residence of the Lieutenant Governor of British Columbia and the ceremonial home of all British Columbians. Government House is located in the heart of the Rockland neighbourhood in Victoria, on the traditional territory of the Songhees and Esquimalt First Nations.

The Lieutenant Governor also offers accommodation to distinguished visitors, including members of the Royal Family, international royalty, heads of state, and other honoured guests of British Columbia.

There have been three Government Houses on this site since 1865. The first official residence, known as Cary Castle, was built in 1859. Six years later it was purchased as the residence of the Governor of Vancouver Island.

When British Columbia entered Confederation in 1871, Cary Castle became Government House, the official office and residence of the Lieutenant Governor of the Province of British Columbia. In May 1899, Cary Castle was destroyed by fire.

Renowned architects Francis Rattenbury and Samuel Maclure were hired to design a new house on the same site. The Rattenbury/Maclure-designed Government House officially opened in 1903. In 1909, a stone porte cochère was added at the request of Lieutenant Governor James Dunsmuir. The House served British Columbia for 54 years until April 15, 1957, when it succumbed to fire. The only thing left standing was the porte cochère. Construction on the new Government House began in December 1957 and closely matched the design of the previous building. The current Government House officially opened on May 19, 1959.

The Conservatory was added in the 1960s as a gift from Lieutenant Governor George Pearkes, and the family of Lieutenant Governor Walter Owens installed the swimming pool in 1978. With the support of the Government House Foundation, successive Lieutenant Governors have left enduring legacies of their time in office. These legacy projects reflect the initiatives and priority programs of each Lieutenant Governor.

Public tours of Government House are scheduled one Saturday a month, starting promptly at 10am and 11am. Admission is free and no booking is required. Please note that there is a maximum capacity of 100 people per tour, so spaces will be allotted on a first come first serve basis

The Cary Castle Mews

The Cary Castle Mews is a cluster of 19th century wooden service buildings located on the southeast side of the Government House estate. The Mews consists of stables, a carriage house, a gaol, a root cellar, a wash house and a poultry house (part of which was later used as a gardener's cottage). These onsite buildings have been used as support buildings to Government House since their construction in the

1870s. Thanks to the efforts of the Government House Foundation, some of the buildings have been rehabilitated and are now outfitted for the public to enjoy.

The Tea House is located in Butterworth Cottage and offers a chance for visitors to enjoy lunch, tea, pastries and other refreshments. Butterworth Cottage was originally built as a poultry barn and in the 1920s was partially adapted as a residence for the head gardener. In 2008, the Cottage underwent further rehabilitation in order to house the Tea House and Interpretive Centre. The Tea Room has become a popular destination for locals and tourists alike. Featuring daily soups, paninis, quiche and other delectables by the Executive Chef at Government House it is the perfect place for lunch, afternoon tea or refreshment during a walk around the Mews and gardens.

The Interpretive Centre is also located within Butterworth Cottage, adjacent to the Tea House in what was originally the poultry barn. Inside the renovated space, visitors will find information about the history of the Estate of the Lieutenant Governor, a designated National Historic Site. Displays include stories and photos of the people who lived and worked in Government House and on the estate, as well as the history of the role of the Lieutenant Governor in British Columbia.

The newly expanded Costume Museum is located in the Carriage House and showcases a large variety of period pieces. From former Lieutenant Governors' uniforms and Chatelaines' dresses to an original butler's uniform, the Museum takes visitors on a sartorial journey through the history of the Estate and Office of the Lieutenant Governor. These historical artifacts are from both the Government House collection and thanks to the generosity of several donors. Visitors to the Costume Museum will also see the historic Landau Carriage on display. In 1901, the Landau was used by the Duke and Duchess of York and Cornwall (later King George V and Queen Mary) on their tour of Victoria and Esquimalt.

The Cary Castle Mews is also home to the Lawrence J. Patten Heraldry Exhibit. This display was created by the British Columbia branch of the Royal Heraldry Society of Canada, whose mission is to promote heraldry, particularly Canadian heraldry, and to encourage an interest in the subject among Canadians. Visitors have the opportunity to learn about the history, design, colour and language of heraldry and view examples of heraldic shields. A preview of the exhibit is available here.

Between the Interpretive Centre and the Carriage House, visitors can also view the original totem pole, Hosaqami. In 1959, the Royal Canadian Navy, as a 50th anniversary event, commissioned artist Chief

Mungo Martin to carve a totem pole and gifted it to the Royal Navy in recognition of the enduring relationship between the two navies. The pole was displayed on Whale Island in Portsmouth, England until the late 1980s, where it was severely damaged by the weather. It was sent back to Canada to see if it could be restored, but the extent of the damage was too much and Chief Tony Hunt, who assisted his father Henry Hunt and his adoptive grandfather Chief Martin in carving the original, recommended it be returned to the earth and a replacement be carved. In celebration of Her Majesty Queen Elizabeth II's Diamond Jubilee in 2012, the Honourable Steven Point and the Government House Foundation commissioned Chief Hunt to carve a replica of the totem pole. The new Hosaqami stands in front of Government House where it remains in perpetuity.

Tea House, Costume Museum and Interpretive Centre Hours:

The Cary Castle Mews will be open for the 2016 season from Tuesday, May 24 to Saturday, September 3, 2016. Tuesday to Saturday, 10am to 4pm.

Location:

1401 Rockland Avenue

Victoria, BC

V8S 1V9

Government House is a 20-minute walk or a five-minute drive from downtown. Free parking is available onsite. Buses on Victoria Regional Transit routes 11 and 14 stop on Fort Street at Joan Crescent, three blocks from Government House.

Haig-Brown House

Haig-Brown Heritage House was the home of Roderick and Ann Haig-Brown between 1936 and 1975. One of British Columbia's most distinguished conservationists, Roderick was a prolific author and a magistrate in Campbell River on Vancouver Island.

Roderick Haig-Brown is perhaps best known for his writings on flyfishing, along with 25 books on natural history and conservation, many novels and essays. In addition to all this, Roderick and Ann were devoted to the protection of BC's rivers, particularly those on which wild salmon are dependent for their survival. Defending the mighty Fraser River from Hydroelectric dams was one of their many successful endeavours.

The Haig-Brown property, including almost 20 acres of forest and farmland, was dedicated as a historic site in 1990. Here the story of the Haig-Browns is presented through house tours, and preserved through continuing restoration of the buildings.

Haig-Brown Heritage House operates as a resource, a museum, a summer bed and breakfast, and a base for a fascinating program of seminars, workshops and regional tours. The garden can be rented for weddings, receptions, and other special events.

The Campbell River flows passed the property and the Haig-Brown Kingfisher Creek enhancement stream runs near the house. Together with the woodlands and the trails, this is an outstanding setting for learning about natural history, flyfishing, gardening, and many other interests that were shared by the Haig-Browns.

Haig-Brown Heritage House is just outside the town of Campbell River, on the east coast of Vancouver Island. The Campbell River Museum is responsible for the overall operations of the Haig-Brown House heritage site.

Contact details:

Haig-Brown Heritage House
2250 Campbell River Road,
Campbell River, BC
V9W 4N7

Tel: 250-286-6646
Fax: 250-286-0109

Hatley Park National Historic Site

Hatley Park in Greater Victoria is Canada's largest and most diverse National Historic site. At the centre of Hatley Park is a magnificent castle built in 1908 by former British Columbia premier and coal baron, James Dunsmuir.

Authentic and beautifully preserved, this 565-acre Edwardian estate is nestled on the southern tip of Vancouver Island, just 25 minutes from downtown Victoria.

Echoes from the past link you to present day adventure as you enjoy a tour of Hatley Castle. Visit the museum, or stroll through the heritage gardens; the Japanese Garden, the Italian Garden, and the Rose Garden. At Hatley Park, amazing things happen!

Visitors can also participate in one of the many visitor programs, or enrol in a garden workshop, attend a special seasonal event, or grab a bite to eat at the Habitat Cafe while visiting Hatley Park National Historic Site.

The intimate setting and gracious hospitality at Hatley Park is ideal for weddings, meetings, retreats, conferences, corporate team building events, motion picture filming, or special events. Hatley Park also hosts the annual Hatley Castle 8K race for runners in February.

Located just 25 minutes from downtown Victoria, in the Westshore community of Colwood, a world of exciting activities awaits you at Hatley Park. As you arrive in the municipality of Colwood, Hatley Park is located at 2005 Sooke Road, on the Island Highway. Look for an elegant rock wall that defines the estate, and a large black sign indicating "Royal Roads University and Hatley Park National Historic Site." Turn on to the property and travel due west towards the water's edge.

Hours of Operation:

Hatley Garden Self Exploration is open daily from 10am to 4pm, and *Guided Walking Estate Tours* are available on a pre-booked basis for groups larger than 10 guests. Shoulder Season runs from October 1 to April 15.

Location & Contact Details:

Hatley Park National Historic Site
Royal Roads University
2005 Sooke Road
Victoria, BC
V9B 5Y2

Tel: 250-391-2666
Fax: 250-391-2620

Helmcken House

Dr. John Sebastian Helmcken set up house in Victoria when he married the daughter of Governor James Douglas in 1852. Originally a three-room log house, the house was built by Helmcken and expanded as both the prosperity and size of the family grew. A surgeon with the Hudson's Bay Company, Helmcken went on to become a statesman and helped negotiate the entry of British Columbia as a province into Canada.

Now the oldest house in British Columbia on its original site that still opens for the public, Helmcken House offers you a fascinating glimpse into the way life was lived over a hundred years ago. The good doctor's original 19th-century medical kit is among the interesting items on display at Helmcken House.

Located in the heart of Victoria's sparkling Inner Harbour district, Helmcken House is surrounded by all the attractions and activity around Victoria's Inner Harbour.

The Royal BC Museum anchors an area bounded by Douglas, Belleville and Government Streets, steps from Victoria's Inner Harbour and across the street from BC's Legislature Buildings. This cultural precinct includes the BC Archives, Helmcken House, St. Ann's Schoolhouse, the

Netherlands Carillon Tower, Thunderbird Park and Mungo Martin House.

Helmcken House is located outside the main entrance of the Royal BC Museum, adjacent to Thunderbird Park. Helmcken House is closed during the fall and winter seasons, including the Halloween period, with the exception of a special Christmas Open House, which is free with a same-day Royal BC Museum admission ticket. Enquire at the museum for further information on the Christmas week at Helmcken House. The grounds of Helmcken House are always accessible when the heritage house is closed.

Contact details:

Helmcken House
c/o Royal BC Museum
675 Belleville Street
Victoria, BC
V8W 9W2
Telephone: 250-356-7226

Point Ellice House

Gold Rush Magistrate and Commissioner Peter O' Reilly acquired Point Ellice House in 1867, and many among the social elite of Victoria gathered at the house.

The flowers in the luxuriant heritage gardens surrounding this rambling Italianate home accurately reflect the family's own notes about their Victorian favourites. The property is like a verdant jewel amid the industries and businesses along the Victoria waterfront.

Overlooking the waters of Victoria's scenic Gorge Waterway, Point Ellice House is, again, where the 'locals' go to enjoy High Tea! And just as British Navy officers and other guests could do over a hundred years ago, you can still be dropped off at the dock! Today you can step aboard the Harbour Ferry in front of the Empress Hotel and take a leisurely tour past Victoria's Old Town on your way to Point Ellice. Of course, you can arrive by land as well!

Point Ellice House is at 2616 Pleasant Street, near the Bay Street Bridge. Approaching from downtown Victoria along Bay Street, travelling west toward the Bridge, turn north on to Pleasant Street where you see the large Point Ellice House sign. (If you're travelling east across the Bridge, a left turn on to Pleasant is not permitted, so proceed to one of the next streets to turn left and loop back to Pleasant) Visitors coming into Victoria from the Swartz Bay Ferry

Terminal need only turn onto Bay Street and watch for the Point Ellice House sign.

Point Ellice House and Gardens: Hours

May 1 June 30: Thursday to Monday, 11am-4pm

July 1 September 6: Open seven days a week, 11am-5pm

September 6 19: Friday to Sunday, 12pm-4pm

September 24 26: 12pm-4pm (Tours only, tea is no longer being served)

November 26 December 19: Friday and Saturday 11am-3pm

Reservations for tea are recommended. Tours and special events can be arranged during the off season.

Contact Details:

Point Ellice House

2616 Pleasant Street,

Victoria, B.C

V8T 4V3

Telephone: 250-380-6506

Royal British Columbia Museum

The Royal British Columbia Museum is a place of discovery. Through three unique galleries, the Museum showcases the human and natural history of British Columbia, and features periodic exhibitions of international renown.

Highly realistic and inviting displays, such as the Ice Age and Coastal Forest dioramas, provide visitors with a sense of having truly experienced the authentic settings of many exhibits.

Travel through the last Ice Age and emerge into British Columbian ecosystems as they exist today. The Natural History Gallery is a fascinating re-creation of our coastal forests and marine environment. You can even visit a live tidal pool for an introduction to sea anemones and starfish! The fascinating and exciting Open Ocean exhibit re-creates a submarine voyage to the depths of the marine world.

The history of British Columbia's First Nations is rich and diverse. Stories of triumph, tragedy and survival are told through a collection of remarkable artifacts, including a ceremonial Big House and totem poles.

Step back in time...from the 1970s to the 1700s. The Modern History Gallery re-creates the growth of British Columbia's industrial society through a realistic setting. Start with a stroll down a cobbled street.

Experience the larger-than-life films at the National Geographic Imax Theatre, located in the Royal B.C. Museum building.

Operated by the Friends of the Royal BC Museum, the Royal Museum Shop and the National Geographic Shop carry quality items that reflect the human and national history of British Columbia. Featuring jewellery, art, publications, calendars, videos, gourmet BC food products and children's items.

Hours of Operation:

Museum: Monday to Sunday 10:00am to 5:00pm (Lobby opens at 9:45am)

IMAX: Monday to Sunday 10:00am to 8:00pm

Closed Christmas Day and New Years Day.

Contact Details:

Royal BC Museum

675 Belleville Street

Victoria, BC

V8W 9W2

Tel: 250-356-7226

Fax: 250-387-5674

Website: **Royal British Columbia Museum**

The Royal British Columbia Museum is located on the Inner Harbour of Victoria on Vancouver Island, opposite The Empress Hotel and the BC Legislative Buildings.

Empress Hotel

The Jewel of the Pacific, The Fairmont Empress Hotel is one of Victoria's highlights. Cresting the city's Inner Harbour, this 477-room hotel was built in the Edwardian style and recently restored to its original grandeur, with antique furniture and luxurious décor.

Considered to be the most photographed attraction on Vancouver Island, The Fairmont Empress was originally designed by Francis Rattenbury, and opened in 1908.

In true British tradition, the hotel is famous for its elegant Afternoon Tea served to over 130,000 visitors annually. Savour tea in the finest tradition, accompanied by fresh seasonal fruit and Chantilly cream, traditional raisin scones with thick Jersey cream, strawberry preserves, sandwiches, pastries and tarts. All served with silver service in the elegant Tea Lobby, stately Harbourside Room, or intimate Library Lounge.

Reservations are required and must be made directly with the hotel, a week or two in advance 250-384-8111. Tables are held for 10 minutes after reservation time. Up to five seatings daily: from 12:00 pm until 5:00 pm. Dress Code: Smart casual. Walking shorts, jeans that are not ripped or torn and running shoes are allowed. Tank tops, sleeveless shirts, "short" shorts or cut-offs are not permitted.

Rising regally on the banks of Victoria's Inner Harbour, The Fairmont Empress is the symbolic centrepiece of Victoria, and conveniently located adjacent to the Victoria Convention Centre, the Legislative Buildings, the Royal BC Museum, and shops and local attractions.

The hotel has long been accustomed to entertaining Hollywood celebrities; Rita Hayworth, Jack Benny, Pat O'Brien, Douglas Fairbanks, Katherine Hepburn, Bob Hope, Bing Crosby, Tallulah Bankhead, Roger Moore, John Travolta, Barbara Streisland, Harrison Ford, and a host of others have passed through its lobby. Shirley Temple arrived accompanied by her parents amid rumors that she had fled from California because of kidnapping threats, a story borne from the presence of two huge bodyguards who took the room opposite hers and always left their door open.

In 1965, there was much debate on whether to tear down what was becoming a faded, dowdy hotel, to make room for a more modern, functional high-rise hotel. One local newspaper warned that, 'Without this splendid relic of the Edwardian era, literally tens of thousands of tourists will never return. This is the Mecca, this is the heart and soul of the city.' The decision was announced on June 10, 1966: The Empress would not be demolished. Instead she would embark on a $4 million campaign of renovation and refurbishment, playfully dubbed 'Operation Teacup.'

The walls of the hotel contain stories of unusual guests and employees. In 1987, a woman wrote about her wonderful stay at The Empress and asked if other guests had received a similar late night visitor: a little girl who had watched over her bed and then floated across the room. There are also the stories of an early 20th-century maid, who shows up now and again on the sixth floor to help with the cleaning.

Throughout its history, The Fairmont Empress has played host to kings, queens, movie stars and distinguished guests from around the world. In 1919, Edward, Prince of Wales, waltzed into the dawn in the Crystal Ballroom an event considered by Victorians to be of such importance that almost 50 years later, the obituaries of elderly ladies would appear under headlines such as, 'Mrs. Thornley-Hall Dies. Prince of Wales Singled Her Out.'

In 1989, over $45 million was spent on the Royal Restoration; all the guest rooms were renovated, and a health club, indoor swimming pool and guest reception were added. With an emphasis on craftsmanship, no attempt was made to give the hotel a new image. Instead, the goal was to restore The Fairmont Empress to her original elegance.

In 2001, the $7 million, 8,000 sq. ft., two-level Willow Stream spa was opened to compliment the hotel in a blend of traditional and contemporary style. Willow Stream features 11 treatment rooms, 5 with exterior views, a Finnish sauna, steam room, Hungarian mineral bath, and a wide range of full-service treatments inspired by the elements and reflective of Victoria's stunning natural surroundings.

The strong emotions The Fairmont Empress evokes in many of her guests and protectors is exemplified in the statement made by an irate gentleman, as workers raised the sign above the front entrance: 'Anyone who doesn't know this is The Empress shouldn't be staying here.'

Tour guides in period costume relate the history of the Empress Hotel every Saturday at 10:00am during the summer, commencing mid to late May. Tickets can be purchased at the Dining reservations desk, 250-389-2727.

Contact Details:
The Fairmont Empress Hotel
721 Government Street

Victoria, BC
V8W 1W5

Tel: 250-384-8111

Craigflower Manor

Craigflower was one of Vancouver Island's first European farming communities, established in 1853 along Victoria's Gorge Waterway. The Puget Sound Agricultural Company, owned by the Hudson's Bay Company, established farms to reduce the need for importing goods from abroad, and to meet the Hudson's Bay Company's obligations to Britain to support colonization. On lands purchased from chiefs of the indigenous aboriginal people, Kenneth McKenzie oversaw construction of a self-sufficient settlement.

Long before the arrival of the Craigflower settlers in the mid-1800s, the Kosapsom families occupied this area, with their people using the Gorge waterway and its adjacent lands for shellfish collection and processing during the 5,000 year period prior to European contact. The descendants of the Kosapsom are the Esquimalt Nation, whose people still harvest shellfish, salmon and herring from the tidal waters that separate the Manor from the Schoolhouse.

The Kosapsom Nation's ancestors left behind ash deposits, the shells from the seafood they ate and used, and tools made from stone and bone. The oldest artifact found so far is a crystal quartz microblade (like a small stone razor blade) dating back approximately 2,500 years. Today, the original Georgian Manor house, partly built on the old H.B.C. post-and-beam design, still stands amid fields and gardens, and across the bridge, the oldest remaining schoolhouse in western Canada gives children re-enactment opportunities to experience Victorian attitudes about schooling!

The two-storey log home is one of the last remaining links to original settlement farms established by the Hudson's Bay Company circa 1850s. It is the third oldest building in British Columbia: only Helmcken House at the Royal BC Museum and Tod House in Oak Bay are older.

Craigflower occupies several open hectares at the junction of Craigflower Road (Old Island Highway 1A, almost parallel with the main Trans-Canada Highway 1) and Admirals Road. It is just a 10-minute drive from downtown Victoria and directly accessible from the Trans-Canada via Admirals Road for those approaching Victoria from Duncan and Goldstream Provincial Park. Craigflower is available year-round for booked tours and groups. Program offerings vary widely to suit the needs of individual tour groups. Daytime and evening programs can be arranged for any day of the week. Please be sure to call in advance for group visits.

Craigflower Manor came close to destruction by fire in January 2009. The source of the fire appeared to be a heater under the stairs. Fire crews were credited for their quick work for containing the flames to a hallway and kitchen on the bottom floor, saving priceless and irreplaceable artifacts from damage in the dining room and living room just metres away.

Alerted by a modern-day fire alarm system, heavy black smoke billowed out of the windows when firefighters from Colwood, Esquimalt and View Royal arrived. Greeted by a fireball when they kicked in the back door, firefighters prevented the flames from entering the walls, where the fire would have traveled unimpeded to the attic and quickly engulfed the entire house.

The province of British Columbia took over ownership of Craigflower Manor and its schoolhouse in 2012 from The Land Conservancy of BC. The Victoria Highland Games Association now rents the historic manor to host special weekend events and attract visitors to tour Craigflower Manor. As the manor is being operated with the aid of volunteers, there are no set museum hours for general public viewing. However, the grounds and ancient Kosapsom Village Site are open year round for self-guided tours.

MacMillan Provincial Park

MacMillan Provincial Park on Vancouver Island is famous for Cathedral Grove, one of the most accessible stands of giant Douglas-fir trees in British Columbia. A stroll on the network of trails meandering through the towering ancient Douglas-firs, some of which are more than 800 years old, can be quite an inspirational experience.

Loop trails on either side of the highway lead awe-struck visitors through the mighty forest stands. The south loop showcases the largest Douglas-fir trees, with the biggest one measuring over 9 metres in circumference. The trail on the northern side of the road winds through groves of ancient Western Red Cedar to the shores of Cameron Lake.

This wondrous display of Douglas-fir, Western Hemlock, Grand fir and Western Red Cedar has been undergoing the restoration of its trails since a severe windstorm damaged several sections of the park in January 1997.

Although visitors will now find many of these huge trees lying on the ground, their value has not diminished. These fallen trees open the canopy to provide light, space, shelter and nutrients for the next generations of plants. Natural regeneration is beginning to restore the Cathedral Grove's pristine beauty, and the park's diversity, making a visit to Cathedral Grove all the more intriguing.

Protests by environmental group have unfortunately failed to stop logging companies clearcutting trees right up to the park boundary, thereby threatening the park ecosystem and destroying the wind barrier so necessary to prevent future blowdowns.

In restoring the trails, sections of some fallen trees were removed, offering a close-up opportunity for the curious to count the annual rings. Determine their age for yourself!

Many species of wildlife use the old-growth forest as their home, including several types of woodpeckers, owls, insects, reptiles, amphibians, deer, elk, black bear and cougar. The Cameron River, which flows through the park, contains rainbow, brown and cutthroat trout.

The well-known forester, H.R. MacMillan, donated the 136 hectares of land in 1944 for the perpetual enjoyment of the public in recognition of the unique stand of trees. The area was established as a provincial park three years later, and expanded in size in the spring of 2005.

Park facilities are limited to pit toilets located on either side of Hwy #4, next to the parking lot. Once you have had your fill of these wonderful trees, you can swim or fish in Cameron Lake, picnic along its shores or hike to neighbouring Little Qualicum Falls Park.

The 157-hectare MacMillan Provincial Park is located on both sides of Pacific Highway 4 on the shores of Cameron Lake, 19 miles (30 km) west of Parksville and 10 miles (16 km) east of Port Alberni on Vancouver Island, British Columbia.

Quw'utsun' Cultural & Conference Centre

The Quw'utsun' Cultural and Conference Centre in Duncan on Vancouver Island is a must-see for admirers of native arts and crafts. The world-class attraction is owned and operated by the Cowichan Tribe, the largest Aboriginal band in British Columbia.

Located on 6 acres of beautiful landscaped grounds along the banks of the Cowichan River, a designated BC heritage river, the native heritage centre offers a truly unique experience, sharing the stories and traditions of the Cowichan people from hundreds of years ago.

It is a world of colour and pageantry, where First Nations talent and pride are abundant. The centre is committed to the culture of warmth and sharing, aspiring to bridge the gaps that exist between cultures and to promote native culture in a positive way.

The Quw'utsun' Cultural and Conference Centre offers an authentic First Nations experience, including interpretive tours, traditional art work, salmon barbeques, displays and live demonstrations, and the Khowutzun Tzinquaw Dancers.

In summer you can watch the creation of the famous Cowichan sweaters as they are hand-knitted in one piece, their unique patterns reflecting the knitter's family designs (some even spin their own wool). The Centre also features an open-air carving shed, where native carvers with handmade tools craft traditional 12- to 20-foot totem poles, each pole representing the carver's interpretation of a tribal design. Visitors may view work in progress as the totem poles take shape.

The excellent art gallery and gift shop offers shopping for genuine Cowichan Sweaters in a variety of styles and patterns, knitted apparel, and hand crafted Coast Salish works and art, including carvings, prints, plaques, blankets, clothing, and jewellery handmade with gold, silver and copper. Visitors can custom order from their selection of totem poles. Shopping items are also available for online purchase through the centre's website.

Authentic native cuisine is offered at the centre's restaurant, the Riverwalk Café, which offers a delicious menu of native food using traditional ingredients such as rabbit, venison, buffalo, and halibut. Each dish is prepared individually and served with a complimentary basket of freshly baked native breads. Enjoy your meal while relaxed on the restaurant's patio along the beautiful Cowichan River.

Conference facilities at the Conference Centre blend the latest in high-tech facilities with the Coast Salish uniqueness that is distinctly Cowichan.

The magnificent hand carved entrance poles and the spectacular riverfront view greet the visitor and create an environment that will make the business at hand a pleasure. Seven rooms are available to meet all needs.

The Quw'utsun' Cultural and Conference Centre and Riverwalk Café are located in Duncan in the Cowichan Valley, a 45-minute drive from both Nanaimo and Victoria. The centre is 5 minutes from the Duncan city centre, just off the Trans-Canada Highway 1.

The Quw'utsun' Cultural and Conference Centre is open year-round. Summer hours are 10:30am to 3:00pm from early June to mid September. From mid September through May the centre accepts group bookings of 15 people or more only, and is available for conferences and catering events. Please contact the booking coordinator for more information.

Contact Details:

Quw'utsun' Cultural & Conference Centre

200 Cowichan Way

Duncan, BC

V9L 6P4

Tel: 1-877-746-8119

Attractions

Beaches

Beaches and Picnic Spots on Vancouver Island

Qualicum Beach, about 7.5 miles (12 km) north of Parksville beside Hwy 19A, gently spreads in front of one of the most pleasant small towns on east side of Vancouver Island. Pause here at any of the numerous beachside pullouts and smell the salt air intermingled with the perfume from the many private and public floral displays. From this point northwards, the pace of Vancouver Island slackens noticeably. Not that the southern portion is any more hurried, it's just that there are more people and more congestion. From here north, there is less traffic, and what habitation there is clings to a narrow coastal plain beside the ocean.

Spider Lake Provincial Park is a small lake located 5 miles (8 km) west of Hwy 19A near Horne Lake. There is a lovely stretch of beach beside the warm, clear waters of the lake, on which no motorized boats are allowed. If you're looking for a respite from travel, spend an hour or two picnicking here at any time year-round; take a dip in summer and toss in a hook if you like smallmouth bass. The lake is indented by a number of bays, particularly at its north end, which makes for quiet exploring in a canoe or rowboat.

The beaches around Comox are usually overlooked by visitors, which is a shame. Take the time to drive east of Hwy 19 as it passes through Courtenay and follow the signs to the BC Ferries terminal in Comox. Miles of sandy shore lead off both north and south of the quiet little coastal town, whose charm has not been overwhelmed by either the nearby Canadian Forces Air Base or the more recent influx of arrivals that south Vancouver Island has experienced.

Kye Bay, 3 miles (5 km) north of Comox off Lazo Road, has a long, sandy beach, as does Goose Spit Regional Park, which noses out into Comox Harbour at the west end of Hawkins Road. Kin Beach Park on Kilmorley Road south of the ferry terminal is a good spot to pass time if you're waiting for a sailing. Texada Island's dark form lies in the strait directly east of Comox, while Denman Island lies to the south.

A broad stretch of sandy beach stands revealed at low tide in Seal Bay Regional Park on Bates Rd. Also called Xwee Xwhya Lug, a place with an atmosphere of serenity, by the Comox Native Band, a 0.6-mile (1-km) walk from the parking area through a forested ravine leads to this wide beach. The Comox Valley Ground Search and Rescue Association publishes a detailed map of the Comox Valley that provides invaluable assistance in finding all of these beaches. It is available throughout the Comox Valley.

As you pass through Campbell River, it's hard not to notice strollers and cyclists meandering along Oyster Bay Shoreline Regional Park, a shoreline bike-and-walking trail with gravel beaches and great views across to Quadra Island. Pulverized oyster shells speckle the gravel with a bright, white hue. The trail winds for much of the distance from the town's southern perimeter to the central harbour, passing the new museum on the hillside above the beach. The occasional picnic table and park bench invite travellers to pull over and join the fun.

As you make your way across the island to the west coast, Hwy 4 passes beside a number of fine locations for picnicking and swimming. You'll find both at the Cameron Lake and Beaufort provincial picnic grounds adjacent to the campground in Little Qualicum Falls Provincial Park. Picnic tables are arranged beside the beach. Strong winds blow here in the afternoon, which attracts windsurfers but definitely deters those in small boats.

You can spend days walking the beaches between Ucluelet and Tofino, and in the process discover why some folks spend their whole lives caught up in the surf and tidal rhythms here. Radar Beach, Long Beach, Combers Beach, and Wickaninnish Beach run successively from north to south and stretch for 15.5 miles (25 km) between Cox and Quisitas Points. Together they comprise the Long Beach Unit of beaches. Radar Beach is rugged and puts up a fight when pummelled by the surf. Exercise great caution within range of the surf anywhere on these beaches.

If you only have a short amount of time, head directly to Long Beach, the most easily accessible and also the longest 6 miles (10 km) long! Depending on the season and the height of the swells in Wickaninnish Bay, not to mention the thickness of the mist, you may see surfers, sea kayakers, cyclists, kite flyers, hackey-sackers, disc tossers, swimmers, joggers, and walkers at play on the hard-packed sand. The scene here is as alive as you want to make it, and there's room to spare. Something about the enormity of Long Beach just makes you goofy.

Take Hwy 4 north towards Tofino. The highway runs beside the beach you'll recognize it on sight. There is parking on the south end at Green Point Campground, as well as at the north end of Long Beach. The short trail that leads from the parking lot at Green Point passes a long row of picnic tables sheltered by the salal and stunted Sitka spruce, and deposits visitors at the halfway point on Wickaninnish Bay. To the north are Radar Beach and Long Beach; to the south are Combers Beachand Wickaninnish Beach.

Rocky headlands bookend Wickaninnish Bay, but south and north of it are four equally beautiful sandy expanses, each with a variation on the overall mood of isolation that characterizes these 'outside' waters. Wreck Beach on Florencia Bay is 3 miles (5 km) long and lies at the south end of the Long Beach Unit. It's easily reached from Hwy 4, 3 miles (5 km) north of the Tofino-Ucluelet Junction. Turn west onto Long Beach Road, then south at the first fork. The Wickaninnish Bay Interpretive Centre lies nearby at the end of Long Beach Road.

Cox Bay, Chesterman, and MacKenzie Beaches lie to the north of the Long Beach Unit, between the northern boundary of Pacific Rim National Park and Tofino. There's public access to each of them, though you'll have to do some backroad driving to find it. A small park on Mackenzie Beach is a good place to begin. Take Mackenzie Beach

Road west of Hwy 4 (Pacific Rim Hwy) and watch for a small roadside parking area and picnic table at the end of the road. Chesterman Beach is reached via Lynn Rd, which loops west from Hwy 4. Cox Bay Beach is reached by following the road to the Pacific Sands Resort west of Hwy 4.

Ucluelet has two beaches in particular that welcome picnickers. A trail leads from Bay St to Big Beach. You'll find picnic tables near the trailhead and then a lengthy walk to the beach. A much shorter approach leads through He-Tin-Kis Park to Terrace Beach near the Amphitrite Point lighthouse at the south end of Peninsula Road. Ahous Beachon Vargas Island, north of Tofino, is now part of a new provincial park. To reach it you must either paddle to the sheltered east side of the island and walk across to it on an old telegraph trail, or brave the swells and head right for the beach itself on the exposed west side of the island.

Once on the beach you'll be able to explore for hours. Small coves filled with blue mussel shells brighten the scene at Ahous Beach. Two small islands offshore stand landlocked to Vargas at low tide and have done battle with the elements for thousands of years; they are windshaped into the appearance of gladiator helmets. An intertidal lagoon fills and empties throughout the day. Depending on the height of the tide, you can cross the mouth of the lagoon to explore farther north along the beach. Be cautious so that your return won't be blocked by high water.

If there's one landscape most associated with oceans, it's beaches. Finding the best ones along the southwestern coast is not difficult, as almost all of them have been protected as provincial parks. Beginning at French Beach, a necklace of sites is strung north to Port Renfrew, where the most fabulous of all Botanical Beach is located. Although they are situated within a fairly narrow range, each one has its own personality.

French Beach Provincial Park, about 14 miles (22 km) west of Sooke, is more protected than the rest from the full force of the ocean by the Olympic Peninsula, on the south side of the Strait of Juan de Fuca. It's also the easiest to reach. You can drive to within a short distance of the beach here, whereas a 10- to 45-minute walk is required to reach the other beaches, depending on the location. A wide swath of lawn fronts this pea-gravel beach where you can picnic, swim, beachcomb, and watch for wildlife. Above all, your attention will be drawn to the pulse of the waves as they break, race up the beach, and grab some gravel to take back with them. The stirring sound of the wind in the trees high above tells you that you've left the inner coast behind.

The hillsides above most beaches here plunge down San Juan Ridge. In Juan de Fuca Provincial Park the trails to China Beach and Mystic Beach are surprisingly steep, whereas those to Sandcut Beach, Sombrio Beach, and Botanical Beach are gentler. Once you reach these beaches, however, it's as if you've suddenly been let in on the action hidden behind the scenes in nearby Victoria. Even at the busiest times you'll have plenty of beach to yourself, though you might be surprised to find how calm the ocean can get for weeks at a time in summer. These are the long, lazy, endless days when the Pacific itself becomes laid-back. It becomes so relaxed that even the signposts take a break.

Although you'll find the approaches to China Beach and Botanical Beach well marked off Hwy 14, others such as Sandcut, Mystic, and Sombrio may be more elusive. Sandcut is 1.2 miles (2 km) south of Jordan River; Mystic is just north of China Beach, and the turnoff for Sombrio is just north of Loss Creek Provincial Park. With the exception of Sombrio Beach, which has its own parking lot downhill from Hwy 14, park beside the highway and follow the trail to the beach.

If you have time to visit only one beach, Sombrio is a standout. A rough road leads downhill from Hwy 14, 11 miles (18 km) south of Port Renfrew, to an open parking space. A well-worn trail leads to the beach in 5 minutes. Until recently, a community of squatters lived here, as this is one of the few beaches where freshwater is guaranteed year-round. You'll have to cross Sombrio Creek and pass through a salal hedge to reach the fine gravel beach. Driftwood is in plentiful supply for use as backrests, picnic tables, and temporary shelters.

A steep trail leads to Mystic Beach, rougher than the one to nearby China Beach but just as enchanting. Plan on 15 minutes to walk to each. Part of the charm of visiting these beaches is admiring the rain forest that thrives in this moist climate. Thick moss coats the forest floor, while wispy strands of Spanish moss trail from the trunks and limbs of second-growth Douglas fir, Sitka spruce, western hemlock, and western red cedar. Salal, Oregon grape, and evergreen huckleberries form much of the underbrush, while in damp areas a variety of ferns adds to the riot of growth that feeds on the nutrient-rich ocean air. Aptly named Mystic Beach conjures an image of foggy mornings, paisley sunsets, and reverberating surf. You'll find that and more here, including twin caves at the north end of the beach that are neat to explore at low tide, along with broad, flat, multihued rock outcroppings covered with a zillion green life forms.

One of the best views anywhere on southern Vancouver Island of the Olympic Mountains occurs along Hwy 14 almost 5 miles (8 km) west of China Beach Provincial Park. To get maximum enjoyment, head a short distance uphill on one of the logging roads that lead off the highway in this vicinity. In a clear-cut, there's nothing to block your view.

The easiest beach to reach by far is that at Jordan River (or River Jordan, as shown on some maps), a small settlement between French Beach and China Beach, and home of the West Coast Surfing Association (also called the Jordan River Surf Club). Hwy 14 makes one of its only approaches to the ocean here before beginning to climb San Juan Ridge once more. You'll find picnic tables here at a small recreation site.

One of the glorious things about the Victoria region is that you can picnic here year-round, something that much of the rest of the province (and rest of the country!) has always envied. Each season has its unique character, and life is always assuming new forms. Spring and fall migrations of birds and fish animate the landscape. Evergreen forests brighten a winter landscape that otherwise lies unveiled once deciduous trees drop their summer foliage. Even snow makes the occasional appearance, though it rarely remains for long. Summer droughts and winter rains determine the songs sung by rivers and creeks.

Without doubt, Sidney Spit on Sidney Island, part of the Gulf Islands National Park Reserve, has the finest beaches of any park in the

Victoria region. The hitch is that visiting this park requires a boat ride from the town of Sidney. Ferry service to Sidney Island runs during summer months; otherwise, you must make your own arrangements to get here. The trip takes 15 minutes one way. There is a charge for adults, with reduced rates for seniors and children ages 12 years and under. Ferry service begins at 9am on weekdays and 10am on weekends. The boat holds 35 passengers and leaves from the Sidney Marina just north of the Beacon St dock.

Island View Beach Regional Park is located on the east side of the Saanich Peninsula in North Saanich. Follow Island View Road east from Hwy 17 a short distance to this gentle cobble- and driftwood-strewn beach. Good views of James and Sidney Islands, and beyond to Mount Baker, make this a pleasant, no-charge alternative to taking the ferry to Sidney Spit. An unbroken string of small islands seem to fold into each other offshore. If you get bored watching the action from the shore, there's wildlife viewing in the open fields behind the beach. The best access to the beach is at the entrance to the park and from the parking lot on the north side of an adjacent private RV park. (Note: The entire beach is public.) Locals use the beach area north of the park fronting Indian reserve land for discreet, clothing-optional tanning. The beach leads a long way north to the tip of Cordova Point.

Several picnic tables stand beneath the spreading trees next to Eagle Beach in Elk/Beaver Lake Regional Park, but visitors will find the sound of traffic on nearby Hwy 17 hard to ignore. A stand of tall Douglas firs shelters North Beach and the beach around Cowquitz Creek at the south end of nearby Beaver Lake from traffic. Picnicking here is much more pleasant. The turnoff from Hwy 17 to Beaver Lake is well marked.

Coles Bay Regional Park, a small park on Saanich Inlet, has a rough, barnacle-covered rock beach typical of the peninsula's west side. Bring along a pair of beach shoes to best enjoy the environment. The water in this deep fjord is always invigorating. The park is located on Inverness Road off Ardmore Drive, a short distance west of Hwy 17A (West Saanich Road).

Three small lakes dot the slopes of Mount Work Regional Park. Depending on your mood, the weather, and the season, freshen up in Durrance or Pease Lake on the north side of the park once you've completed the hike to the top of the mountain, or just relax at lakeside and enjoy the woodland ambience. Fork Lake lies at the south end of the hiking trail to the summit of Mount Work. To reach Durrance Lake, take Wallace Dr west of Hwy 17A, then follow Willis Point Road until the lake appears on its north side. Pease Lake is a short distance father west. Follow Willis Point Road to Ross Durrance Road and head south to the lake. Fork Lake is reached by following Millstream Road north of Hwy 1 west of Victoria, then turning northeast on Munnis Road.

Thetis Lake Regional Park lies on the west side of Victoria, about 7 miles (12 km) from the city centre in View Royal. Sandy beaches front the park's two heavily indented lakes, which are connected by a thin canal. If you have a canoe or kayak, you can reach some of the more remote beaches; otherwise, enjoy yourself within an easy walk of the parking lot. To reach Thetis Lake, head west of Victoria on Hwy 1 and watch for signs that point the way north of the highway to the park. Note: Although several hiking trails originate from Thetis Lake Road, the beach is reached by following West Park Lane, about 6 miles (10 km) from the city centre.

Witty's Lagoon Regional Park west of Victoria offers yet another perspective on the coastline. A long swath of sandy beach curves gently along Strait of Juan de Fuca, protecting a crucial marshland from the full force of waves and wind. Find a sturdy piece of driftwood and shelter from the constant breeze, which even in summer has a fresh edge to it. From this vantage point, you can look across the strait to the towering heights of the Olympic Mountains in Washington and its signature glaciated formation, Hurricane Ridge. The shallow beach makes for a pleasant warm-water swim after the tide rises over sun-heated rocks. There are several entrances to the park. For quick access to the beach, take Hwy 14 west of Victoria, then turn south on Metchosin Road. The well-marked trailhead at Sitting Woman Falls is located opposite the Metchosin Golf Course. Allow 10 to 15 minutes to walk from the parking lot to the beach.

Sooke Potholes Provincial Park is located north of Hwy 14 and just east of Sooke. The Galloping Goose Trail runs past this small day-use park. Swimming in the potholes that have been carved in the sandstone in the Sooke River provides ideal refreshment on hot summer days. This site has been luring picnickers from the Victoria region for years, so don't be surprised by the controlled mayhem when you arrive. Picnic tables line the river next to the parking area, and the potholes are just steps beyond.

Beaches and Picnic Spots on the Southern Gulf Islands

As you explore from island to island, you'll find dozens of small beaches along the convoluted shorelines. While all shoreline is public land in British Columbia, not all of it is easily reached, nor does much of it provide a pleasant place to relax while watching the ebb and flow of the tides. Here's a sampling of some of the best and most readily accessible places in the Southern Gulf Islands.

One of the prettiest beaches on all the islands is at Ruckle Provincial Park on Saltspring Island. A trail leads down to the secluded beach from the nearby campground. It's easy to imagine generations of island families making their way here on hot summer days when the Ruckle farm was in full swing. A tall forest surmounts the beach, much of it sturdy first-growth Douglas fir, but there are also a number of hardwood species planted by the Ruckles that are a delight come fall. This beach is a wonderful refuge from the outside world, a place to find a sturdy piece of driftwood for a backrest and relax.

Drummond Park at the head of nearby Fulford Harbour has a more exposed pebble beach to explore. Look for the ancient pictograph image carved in the face of one of the larger boulders on the beach. Although the wooded setting at Weston Lake, about 2 miles (3 km) north of Fulford Harbour, is less picturesque than by the ocean, there is a sandy beach here where you can enjoy a freshwater swim.

One of the best beaches on the Pender Islands is at Mortimer Spit, close to the canal between the two islands. A snout of sand where you'll find plenty of room and few visitors to share the beach with juts out into Navy Channel. A more popular spot is just north at Hamilton

Beach at Port Browning. You'll find a more festive atmosphere here in summer with a pub, marina, cafe, and picnic tables beside the beach. On the far shore, visible from Hamilton, is a sandy strip of beach at Razor Point. Take Bedwell Bay Road south from the ferry dock at Otter Bay to reach Hamilton Beach. Follow Razor Point Road east of Port Browning to find the small beach on the point.

If you take the time to travel to the very end of South Pender Island, you'll find the small beach park at Gowlland Point Park, the prettiest of all the beaches on the two Penders. A pebble beach slopes down to an indented shoreline. During winter storms, which pound this exposed coast with regularity, the ocean moves the cobblestones around with percussive effect. From the beach, you look due south into the San Juan Islands, west across the Strait of Juan de Fuca to Hurricane Ridge on Washington State's Olympic Peninsula and east to Saturna Island's Monarch Head, with Mount Baker rising above the mainland. To reach the park from the ferry dock, follow Bedwell Bay, Canal, Spalding, and finally Gowlland Point Road to its southern terminus. If you want solitude, this is where to find it.

Much of the beach at Miners Bay on Mayne Island is composed of a gently sloping shelf of smooth rock. At low tide much of this table rock is revealed and makes for interesting exploration. Miners Bay is the commercial hub of Mayne Island and is anchored by the historic Springwater Lodge. Make your way from the ferry dock along Village Bay Road, an easy walk or bike ride. A beautiful sand-and-pebble beach is located on Mayne Island's east side at Campbell Bay. The trail leading down to the beach is not well marked but isn't difficult to locate. Follow Georgina Point Road east of Miners Bay to its junction with Waugh Road. Head south on Waugh, and as the road rounds Campbell Bay, watch for a shady trail that runs down the embankment to the ocean below. An overhanging forest shades the beach, providing a cool place to relax out of the sun. Big pieces of driftwood sit mired in the sand, ready to prop you up to enjoy the view as you look due east across the strait towards Vancouver.

Beaches and Picnic Spots on the Discovery Islands

Even though there are no public campgrounds on some islands, there are attractive parks especially for picnickers, located where you can take best advantage of the seaside environment. Whether you're on the island just for the day or have made arrangements for private overnight accommodation, you'll want to head for these places to complement your visit.

Every island is invested with magic. Those who visit Hornby Island have really bought into the dream, as it takes two ferries to reach.

Once there, head for the picnic grounds at Tribune Bay Provincial Park or Helliwell Provincial Park. The latter sits on a headland forested with a beautiful stand of old-growth Douglas fir. If you arrive here in spring you'll be treated to a dazzling wildflower display. The rewards of visiting later in summer are the huckleberries and dark blue salal berries that cloak the hillside above the beach. Tribune Bay boasts eroded hoodoo formations and a sandy beach that vies with any in the Gulf Islands as the most ideal place to frolic and swim.

You'll get to tour Quadra Island on the way to your picnic in Rebecca Spit Marine Provincial Park. The park lies on the east side of the island at sheltered Drew Harbour, almost 6 miles (9 km) from the ferry landing at Quathiaski Cove. There are more picnic tables here than on any other island, and a prettier sandy beach than almost anywhere else on Quadra. Anglers launch from the ramp here, and it's a good place to pick up word on the health of fish stocks.

Cortes Island is blessed with both a provincial campground at Smelt Bay and a sublime picnic and fishing location at Mansons Landing Marine Provincial Park. If they aren't biting in the saltchuk ('chuk' is a Native word for water) just turn your attention to the fish in Hague Lake, a freshwater lake located within the park, a rarity in the Marine Provincial park system. A wide, sandy beach beckons to those who just wish to spread a blanket beside a driftwood backrest and dig into the cooler.

For those who journey the length of Lasqueti Island, there's picnicking and swimming at Squitty Bay Provincial Park, 9 miles (15 km) south of the ferry dock at False Bay. You'll be ready to drink from the freshwater pump by the time you arrive here. Picnic tables are arrayed among the spray-shaped forest of Douglas fir and strawberry arbutus (madrona). This idyllic location overlooks two narrow coves where the water is clear, green, and warm in summer months. A portion of the park is fenced off to protect it from the feral sheep that graze all over the island. Years ago, a small meadow was cleared above the beach at Squitty Bay, where there are still signs of a old orchard.

Without doubt, the best beaches in the entire inland sea are found on Savary Island offshore from Lund on the Sunshine Coast. Unfortunately, few visitors travelling without a boat will get the opportunity to stroll them. Savary is not serviced by public ferry so transportation is limited to water taxi or airplane. If you do have a boat, kayak, or canoe, the First or Second Beaches on the island's north side are the easiest to reach. It's debatable which side of the snout-shaped island has the best beaches when you're in heaven, it doesn't matter which side of the street you walk on.

Festivals & Events on Vancouver Island

Vancouver Island celebrates some fabulous annual festivals, carnivals, events, and outdoor recreation competitions. Time your visit to Vancouver Island to coincide with some remarkable natural spectacles of the animal kingdom, outdoor music recitals, local art fairs, and natural or historical exhibitions or just come along and stare at the crazy things people do for work and pleasure. Vancouver Island offers a wonderfully rich and colourful array of local festivities, entertainment, and outdoor pursuits.

Victoria Film Festival (February)
The Victoria Film Festival is a selection of films that they scoured the earth to find that you might not normally have a chance to see. The organizers bring the films together for a ten-day celebration, and often the filmmakers come to join in. Not only do you get to see some of the best films of the year, you get to hear what the filmmaker has to say. Lots of people buy Film Passes to see films everyday during the festival, or they pick up the discount 5-Film or 10-Film ticket packages. For more information visit: www.victoriafilmfestival.com

Pacific Rim Whale Festival (mid March to early April)
The northward migration of an estimated 21,000 Gray whales along the west coast of Vancouver Island has heralded the coming of spring

for thousands of years. Grays travel close to shore, pausing to feed in shallow waters, providing excellent viewing opportunities from strategic shore locations. The greatest number of whales can be seen in the spring, although many whales remain in local waters to feed until the return migration to Mexico in October. Besides the unique opportunity of seeing these huge mammals, ocean scientists and whale researchers present education programs about whale migration, biology and the conservation efforts that have brought the Gray whales back from the edge of extinction. If you want a closer look at these magnificent animals, venture out onto the open Pacific aboard local charter boats offering scheduled whale watching tours from Tofino or Ucluelet.

For more information visit: Pacific Rim Whale Festival

Brant Wildlife Festival (April)

The Brant Festival is held in Parksville and Qualicum Beach in early April each year to celebrate the migratory stopover of over 20,000 Brant geese. Each spring, immense flocks of Brant geese descend on the shores of Vancouver Island for a last major food stop before continuing their amazing journey north to the Alaskan breeding grounds. The communities of Parksville and Qualicum Beach celebrate this wonderful natural event with the three-day Brant Festival that includes nature talks, guided tours of marsh, forest and seaside

habitats, photography workshops and a birding competition.
For more information visit: www.brantfestival.bc.ca

Swiftsure Sailing Race (May)

A fleet of the most competitive racing sailboats converges on Victoria for the annual Swiftsure race, the longest-running yacht race in the Pacific Northwest. The challenge, hosted by the Royal Victoria Yacht Club, attracts around 200 boats in the short, middle and long-distance events that take competitors out and across the Juan de Fuca Strait and back, providing spectators with a colourful display of boats and spinnakers.
For more information visit: www.swiftsure.org

Great Walk (June)

North America's toughest pledge walk 63-1/2 kilometres along gravel forestry roads in some of the most rugged and beautiful country in the world. The annual walkathon between Tahsis and Gold River attracts thousands of outdoor enthusiasts to raise money for charity.
For more information visit: www.greatwalk.com

Jazz Fest International (June)

Lovers of jazz can take in music by jazz performers from around the world when they grace Victoria's stages for 10 days and nights in June. Various indoor and outdoor venues in downtown Victoria host the festival as the city heats up with more than 250 of the world's best jazz, blues and world beat artists.

For more information visit: www.jazzvictoria.ca

Nanaimo Marine Festival (July)

Visitors won't want to miss the world-famous Bathtub Race held during the Nanaimo Marine Festival in late July. Men and women of all ages and backgrounds come from around the world to race across the Georgia Strait in bathtubs, from Nanaimo to Vancouver. Competitors always take the 48-km run very seriously, but the day is filled with tons of fun and laughs for both contestants and spectators alike. Hundreds of outboard powered "tubbers" plane their zany craft at high speed across the strait in their quest for the much-coveted first prize.

For more information visit: Loyal Nanaimo Bathtub Society

Filberg Festival (August)

The Filberg Festival, reputed to be the best Arts and Crafts festival in the Pacific Northwest, offers an amazing selection of the finest quality work by BC resident artists, from pottery to handmade toys. This outdoor show and sale is displayed in the gardens of Comox Valley's historic Filberg Lodge. Entertainment is local too, provided in many musical styles.

For more information visit: www.filbergfestival.com

Victoria Fringe Festival (September)

Over the Labour Day weekend theatre troupes from our own backyard and around the world present entertaining performances at different venues all over Victoria. For the very best in comedy, drama, dance, magic, music, story telling and more, the Fringe is the best ticket in town.

For more information visit: www.victoriafringe.com

Symphony Splash (August)

One of the grandest events in Victoria's summer season is the annual Symphony Splash. The Victoria Symphony Orchestra performs on a floating stage secured in Victoria's beautiful Inner Harbour. The free show traditionally climaxes with a resounding rendition of Tchaikovsky's 1812 Overture amidst a dazzling display of fireworks and booming cannons.

For more information visit: www.victoriasymphony.ca

Victoria Dragon Boat Festival (August)

Spectacular dragon boats roar into Victoria's Inner Harbour, providing a colourful spectacle, with organized entertainment onshore.

For more information visit: www.victoriadragonboat.com

Royal British Columbia Museum

The Royal B.C. Museum in Victoria is one of the foremost cultural institutions in the world, and always manages to produce remarkable annual feature exhibitions.

For more information visit: Royal BC Museum

Victoria Classic Boat Festival (September)

Victoria's picturesque Inner Harbour is the place to be on the Labour Day weekend, when around 100 classic sail and power boats from throughout the Pacific Coast and beyond arrive for the Victoria Classic Boat Festival. The festival is one of the Pacific Coast's most celebrated displays of heritage sail and power craft, open to vessels of traditional plank-on-frame construction built prior to 1956, or newer vessels that are built to pre-1956 designs.

Visit: www.classicboatfestival.ca

Hot Springs

Vancouver Island has a number of hot springs, one of which Hot Springs Cove is considered to be the finest in Canada. The hotsprings on Vancouver Island are situated in some of the most scenic and natural areas in British Columbia, with no development around them, so visiting them is an adventure in itself. The two main hot springs are reached by boat or floatplane on the rugged west coast of Vancouver Island, with access from Tofino.

Hot Springs Cove

Hot Springs Cove is a splendid hot spring still enjoyable in its natural state, located in Maquinna Provincial Park in the remote northern end of Clayoquot Sound. The boiling spring water bubbles up from deep in the earth and cascades down a small cliff into a series of natural layered rock pools, cooled by the incoming Pacific Ocean surf. The spring water is very hot, and is clear with just a faint smell and taste of sulphur.

Ahousat Hot Springs

Tofino provides access to a second, cooler spring at Ahousat Hot Springs, located on the shores of Matilda Inlet in Gibson Marine Provincial Park, on the south side of Flores Island. Ahousat Hot Springs is a natural warm spring, considered to be of therapeutic value, that bubbles up into a concrete tank. The spring water is clear and tasteless, with just a faint smell of sulphur, and has a maximum temperature of 25° C (77°F).

Other hot springs reported to be on Vancouver Island include; springs on the Mate Islands, the small group of islands located across from Hot Springs Cove; a hot spring in Kyuquot Sound, close to Fair Harbour; hot springs near the lower rapids of the Kennedy River, near

Tofino; and Pipesteam Inlet, on the north shore of Barkley Sound north of the Broken Group Islands.

Kid's Stuff on Vancouver Island and BC Gulf Islands

Vancouver Island offers a range of activities and attractions that will keep everyone entertained and excited it's a children's paradise! Don't waste a perfectly sunny day inside, as there are many parks and sights to explore! Yes, it does rain here, which is why the trees are tall and the gardens so lush rain or no rain, there's no shortage of things to do.

Greater Victoria

Just a short walk south of downtown Victoria is Beacon Hill Park, with its manicured gardens and many attractions. Park facilities include walking trails, a wading pool, water fountains, picnic areas, monuments, sports fields and playgrounds, a band pavilion, and what was once the world's tallest totem pole. Top of the list for kids and adults alike is the Beacon Hill Children's Farm; lots of baby animals, pot belly pigs, zebu, miniature horses and other critters to meet and pet and don't miss the goat stampede at closing time!

Victoria Bug Zoo: Discover the amazing world of insects at this unusual and fascinating zoo on Courtney Street there's even an ant farm!

While the Maritime Museum of BC will have the pirates in search of treasure, a visit to Lasercity Fun Centre on View Street for laser tag will get the kid's hearts pumping.

The whole family can enjoy an IMAX film at the National Geographic Theatre, next to the Royal British Columbia Museum in downtown Victoria (corner Government and Belleville Streets). Plan a morning or afternoon to experience this museum, where you can see what it was like in the gold rush days much of BC's history is captured here.

Miniature World at the Empress Hotel is well worth a visit, for adults to put things back into a kid's perspective. There are over 80 attractions for the whole family, including the world's smallest operational sawmill a miniaturized extravaganza that continues to thrill and delight the young and young at heart. Visit Miniature World's Wonderful World of the Circus and return to those nostalgic days when the circus came to town. Feel the magic, the wonderment of the Grand City Parade, the Big Top, the Wild Beasts and the death defying High Wire Acts.

Horse drawn carriages take you on various tours around many of Victoria's exciting sites and sounds. From the beautiful Inner Harbour and the Ivy Covered Empress hotel and our magnificent Parliament

Buildings to many notable Heritage Homes, through Beacon Hill park and much much more.

Llamas are friendly and delightful animals that bring joy to all who are graced by their presence. With their long, silky eyelashes framing big, intelligent eyes, llamas find their way into the lives of many people. There are a number of Llama farms and Llama bed & breakfasts in the area that offer Llama Walks and Llama Hiking.

Stroll amid lush vegetation at the fascinating Victoria Butterfly Gardens at 1461 Benvenuto Avenue in Central Saanich, an indoor tropical garden filled with hundreds of dazzling free-flying exotic butterflies and colourful birds.

Trails: Whether you enjoy hiking, cycling, roller blading, horseback riding, or just going for a stroll, Victoria and the Saanich Peninsula boasts some superb trails, including the Galloping Goose Trail, the Lochside Trail, and other great peninsula trails. The combination of the Galloping GooseTrail and the Lochside Trail creates a safe trail all the way from Downtown Victoria to the Swartz Bay ferry terminal north of Sidney.

If you're looking for a great beach, try Willows Beach in Oak Bay. Farther along Beach Drive, past Uplands, there is also Cadboro Bay Beach. The sea air, playgrounds, and sandy beaches are sure to melt away any worries and delight both young and old. Visit the Oak Bay Marina to see the antics of harbour seals in their natural habitat. All Fun Recreation Park in Langford offers a Go Kart Raceway, a Moto Cross track, Batting Cages, an Ice Cream Parlour, and 18 holes of adventure Mini Gol. Also on site is Western Speedway.

Stroll through peaceful meadows at Fort Rodd Hill National Historic Park, overlooking Esquimalt Harbour in Colwood, a coastal artillery site built to defend Victoria and the Esquimalt Naval Base operational from 1878 to 1956. Located on the large grounds of Fort Rodd Hill is Fisgard Lighthouse, the first lighthouse on Canada's rocky west coast, built in 1860 by the British when Vancouver Island was still a crown colony.

The town of Sidney is home to family attractions as well. The Shaw Ocean Discovery Centre is an aquarium and marine education centre showcasing the extraordinary marine life and amazing ecosystem in the waters surrounding the Gulf Islands and the Salish Sea. From microscopic plankton to Puget Sound King crabs, wolf eels to giant Pacific octopus, the vast aquatic exhibits fascinate visitors of all ages. With 87 tonnes of sea water and 17 habitats, the Centre's ever-changing seascapes and touch pools offer an unforgettable and unique hands-on, hands-wet experience that reveals the mysteries of the ocean to all ages. Located on the waterfront in Sidney. Open daily from 10:00 am to 4:30 pm.

Discover the incredible world of gems and minerals at Mineral World and Scratch Patch in Sidney. A very popular attraction for children, the Scratch Patch is an outdoor adventureland designed to turn anyone into an enthusiastic rockhound. Pick and choose from millions of beautiful semi-precious stones and tropical shells, or try panning for gold!

The ocean around Vancouver Island abounds with spectacular marine life, you can see these magnificent creatures up-close; whale watching tours with marine naturalists are a "must do" for any visitor to Victoria. Sidney is also a good spot for this popular activity.

South Vancouver Island

The British Columbia Forest Museum located in Duncan portrays the history of BC's forestry industry through indoor and outdoor exhibits. Board the steam locomotive that travels through a turn-of-the-century farmyard and a logging camp.

Explore the sculpted sandstone tidepools at the world-famous Botanical Beach in Juan de Fuca Provincial Park, a wonderful place for appreciating marine biology and viewing intertidal life it's a thrill to experience.

Central Vancouver Island

Between Parksville and Qualicum Beach is Morningstar Farm, home to Little Qualicum Cheeseworks and MooBerry Winery. There are many things to do on this heritage dairy farm: see how they make that yummy cheese, visit the farm animals, have a picnic and take a self-guided tour. Parents can shop in the FarmGate store and taste some wine and cheese samples!

If you want to take the kids underground, there are several hundred significant caves on Vancouver Island, including those at Horne Lake Caves Provincial Park. From education family oriented tours to deep dark adventure, these caves offer something for everyone.

Strathcona Park Lodge and Outdoor Education Centre is committed to helping children of all ages appreciate the wilderness. Within a supportive environment, climb a rock bluff, rappel on a rope, swing on a zip-line and co-operatively solve problems on a ropes course. Learn survival techniques, canoeing, kayaking, orienteering and wilderness etiquette; then participate in a canoe journey for an optional overnight camp-out. Natural history discussions are stimulated while exploring a sphagnum bog, home of insectivorous sundew.

Pacific Rim / West Coast of Vancouver Island

Along the island's West Coast, the Wickaninnish Centre is a definite highlight for all ages. The centre's purpose is to provide an understanding of the North Pacific Ocean and its influence on nature and man. The history of the North Pacific coast is illustrated by a collection of artifacts used by Nuu-chah-nulth Indians, and interpretive displays.

The Whale Centre Maritime Museum offers a display of artifacts collected and donated by Tofino locals over the past twenty five years. On exhibit is an assortment of traditional native jewelry, cedar baskets, paddles, sea life, local artifacts from traditional whaling equipment to original navigation charts of the area and a complete 40' gray whale skeleton.

Llama Walks and Llama Hiking

Llamas are friendly, delightful and extremely intelligent animals that carry themselves with serene pride. These beautiful animals are of gentle disposition, easy to train and unfazed by people. With their long, silky eyelashes framing big, intelligent eyes, llamas find their way into the lives of many people, in many walks of life, bringing joy to all who are graced by their presence.

Llamas are a herd animal, curious, sensitive, aloof and independent. Many enjoy being scratched or rubbed and spending time with their owners. They can become companions, packers, pull a cart, enter shows and parades, entertain at nursing homes and schools, and golfers think it's great fun to have a llama caddy. Llamas come in a rainbow of colours and shades markings can be in a variety of patterns, from solid to spotted. They don't spook, kick or bolt, and are safe with children. Llamas greet you with a soft sniffing and blowing in your face. The best way to greet a llama is quietly with your hands behind your back and offering your face for inspection. Stand still and let the gentle natured llama approach you.

Llamas are very quiet animals. Humming is their primary means of vocal expression. A llama's hum sounds similar to a person's hum. Depending upon the situation, llamas may also cluck, orgle or make an alarm call. All sounds are very distinctive and easily recognizable. It will be clear what llamas are trying to express if you look at their situation and listen.

Llamas live for about twenty years and are easy to maintain. They need a three-sided structure providing shelter from wind, rain, snow and hot sun. Other needs include fresh water and hay, safe fencing and pasture, adequate room to exercise, and most need their toenails trimmed twice yearly.

All llamas are normally trained to calmly accept a halter and lead, load into a trailer, truck or van, accept brushing and shearing, and allow their feet to be handled for trimmings. The llama gestation period is between 335 and 360 days, with 350 days used as a rule of thumb. Baby llamas are called crias, which can be weaned from their mothers at six months.

Vancouver Island has approximately 40 llama farms, with 4 of them located in the Greater Victoria area. Llama farms are becoming increasingly popular, and Bed and Breakfasts located on llama farms add an extra dimension to an already pleasant stay in British Columbia. These lodgings allow guests the exciting opportunity of taking the llamas on quiet walks on nearby trails.

Charismatic llamas have a therapeutic effect on visitors, and it would seem that guests just can't get enough of them. They feed them, photograph them, cuddle them, and sit, talk and walk with them. It's nearly impossible to sit quietly with a llama and not find yourself engaged in their special magic. Llamas are to love, to enjoy, and to relax and have fun with.

Do llamas spit?

Usually llamas spit to tell another llama to get out of their space or food. A bred female will spit at males who are trying to approach her, and some llamas will spit at others getting too close to their crias. Rarely will llamas spit at their owners. If they do, it is usually in fear or pain and often means the handler is at fault. Spitting at humans is the exception not the rule.

Llamas For Therapy

Llamas instinctively learn to be quiet and gentle with the weak or handicapped, making them great therapy animals. They are naturally curious and alert, have beautiful, large eyes and interact with a new person with a genuine interest. Llamas seem to have a certain sense that some people are special, and don't react negatively to cumbersome movements or unusual speech, which is why handicapped people respond so positively to llamas. Some doctors have recommended the use of llamas with high stress patients who need to relax, and others are using llamas in therapy work with handicapped adults and children. Llamas have also been recommended by psychologists and doctors as stress reducers for people with very active lives.

Llamas For Packing and Trekking

The llamas' ability as a pack animal has been rediscovered by hikers and forest work crews in mountainous areas and wilderness parks in North America. Capable of carrying 50 to 100 pound packs and travelling 10 to 15 miles a day, llamas are agile and blessed with common sense. Being smaller than most pack animals, and with their padded feet, llamas have minimal impact on the backcountry environment and require far less to drink. The llamas' unique two-toed foot, with a broad leathery pad on the bottom and curved nails in front, makes them remarkably sure-footed on a variety of terrains, including sandy soil, rock and snow. Thanks to the easygoing nature of the llamas and by helping with the load, llamas can open up the wilderness to day-long treks or overnight camping for those whose fitness may prevent them from carrying their own equipment, allowing a one-on-one relationship with their pack companion. Llamas can also be trained to pull carts and wagons.

Lamas in Education

Many llama projects educate young people in the raising, breeding and training of llamas. The unique and gentle nature of the llama nurtures the growth of children's self esteem and allows them to share their knowledge and companionship through nursing home and school visits, parades, and other community events.

Llama Fibre

One of the most treasured by-products of llamas is their exquisite fibre. Llamas have wonderful fine fibre that is soft and warm, sheds rain and snow, and rarely shrinks when washed. Hand spinners, knitters and weavers all appreciate the softness and warmth of llama fibre, creating beautiful garments. The variety of natural colours and the absence of lanolin are other desirable qualities. Llamas can be shorn annually or biannually depending on preference and growth rate. Llama fleece normally grows 3 to 4 inches per year with a full grown coat averaging 5 to 10 pounds. Llama fibre can range from short to long, coarse (good for bags, rugs, felting and ropes) to extremely fine (wonderful for sweaters, hats and scarves) and has a tensile strength and durability three times stronger than a wool strand.

Llamas As Guards

Llamas have proven themselves to be marvellous guardians of livestock. The effective use of llamas as sheep guards began in North America in the early l980s, with more than half of the llamas guarding sheep achieving a 100% rate of success, completely eliminating losses. Many livestock farms have successfully used llamas to guard flocks of 200 to 1,000 meat, wool and milk producing animals in all types of terrain and pastures sizes. Guard llamas work well in teams of two. The value of livestock saved each year often exceeds the purchase cost and annual maintenance of the llama.

Llamas for show

These intelligent animals are judged for conformation, balance, structure and performance. Showing llamas has become a favourite family affair now that hundreds of llama events are held across Canada and the United States. Today the show circuit is enhanced with local, regional, and national shows.

Llama History

Archaeological evidence indicates that the llama and alpaca were domesticated in Peru about 6,000 years ago. One theory suggests that the llama was domesticated from the wild guanaco, and the smaller alpaca from the wild vicuna. In pre-Inca times, certainly by the 11th century AD, sophisticated breeding and management systems were preserving and perpetuating the integrity of the subspecies breeding animals of supreme quality, ideally suited to their various purposes. The Incas placed prime emphasis on alpaca breeding, as at that time fibre and textiles were of great economic importance. The llama had been bred for use as a beast of burden in addition to their fine fibre. In the late 1800s and early 1900s, private animal collectors and zoos reintroduced them to their original North American homeland.

Maritime Museum of British Columbia

The Maritime Museum of British Columbia is a principal maritime museum on the Pacific Coast of Canada, and one of the major maritime museums on the West Coast of North America. The museum is housed in the historic 1889 Provincial Law Courts building situated in Bastion Square in Victoria BC. Experience British Columbia's maritime heritage and discover the inspirational stories that create BC's amazing culture.

NOTE: The Maritime Museum of BC is in the process of moving from Bastion Square to a new location in Victoria, and will remain closed throughout 2015.

Visitors can explore an exciting world of BC maritime history, starting with these permanent museum exhibits.

Explorers and Navigation

The fog-shrouded Pacific Coast of North America has a deep and rich heritage that spans the centuries from the first aboriginal cultures to European exploration and early settlement. Initially isolated from the European world, this region witnessed the navigation feats of early mariners and the clash of empires. Meet great characters such as Captains James Cook and George Vancouver, witness the territorial see-saw between Russia, the United States and British Canada, and discover the many mysteries of the Pacific Coast. Be sure to inspect the navigation instruments that made the exploration and surveys of the West Coast possible, and find out why there are so many Spanish place names.

Pirates

While pirates and privateers played a minor role in the history of the West Coast, they assume a large place in the imaginations of many. At the Maritime Museum of BC, you will have the opportunity to encounter these scallywags of the sea, and learn the differences between buccaneers, pirates and privateers. Hint: One of them has a legal right to steal guess which one! Make time to check out the fierce-looking weapons used in sea battles, and inspect the horrific gibbet (human cage) that was the fate of many watery criminals.

The Fort and The City

In 1843, the great fur-trading Hudson's Bay Company moved its operations north from the Columbia River to an isolated spot on the southern tip of Vancouver Island. The trading post that started as a wooden palisade fort would grow to become the vibrant city of

Victoria that we know today. Victoria had many advantages, such as a fine natural harbour, and benefited as a veritable storehouse, supplying miners bound for the Fraser River, Cariboo and Klondike gold rushes. The economic and social life of Victoria was also greatly influenced by the presence of the Royal Navy Pacific Fleet and by the Royal Canadian Navy after 1910.

Shipbuilding

Shipbuilding on Vancouver Island had its origins as a repair station for ships in need, far from their home ports. Over the years, a vibrant shipbuilding and engineering industry flourished, with boat yards turning out everything from large sailing vessels to coastal steamers and even pleasure craft. Following the boom periods during the two world wars, shipbuilding activities greatly declined. Explore the many strange looking tools used by shipbuilders and marvel at the skills needed to tie complicated rope knots and create floating beauty in wood or metal.

Whaling and Fishing

From the earliest aboriginal occupation, the extremely rich sea life of the Pacific Coast has provided food and other valuable products. Fish, seals and whales were harvested in huge numbers, and in the process helped to shape the economy and settlement of the coast. Today, whales and seals are no longer hunted, but the commercial fishing industry is still the lifeblood of many communities. Did you know that salmon has always been a prime resource on the West Coast, with the first smoked fish being exported to Hawaii in the 1830s? Don't miss the massive cannon used to harpoon whales in Pacific waters!

Tilikum

In 1901, Captain John Voss and his partner, Norman Luxton, set sail from Victoria to circumnavigate the globe. What set their feat apart is that their 38-foot craft, the Tilikum, was transformed into a sailing craft from a native canoe fashioned from a single cedar log. Overcoming many obstacles, and with sterling sailing skills, Voss steered this strange boat around the world to reach London, England, in 1904. The best part of this story is that you can actually see the Tilikum in the Maritime Museum of BC. Yes, after wandering the world's oceans, the famous sailing canoe came back to its home in Victoria.

Crow's Nest

What was it like to work and live aboard a huge wooden sailing vessel? Well, young visitors can experience this first-hand by joining its crew and exploring the crow's nest. Kids are encouraged to climb the ratlines, steer a course, and fire off a few volleys from the swivel cannon located on the large mock-up of a ship's deck.

Shipwrecks

The rugged coastline of British Columbia is treacherous for marine navigation, and countless ships have ended up in peril. Perhaps the worst naval disaster was the Princess Sofia, a coastal steamer that went down off Alaska in 1918, with the loss of all 343 people on board. The story of the Sofia and other unlucky ships makes chilling reading and reminds us of the fierceness of the sea.

Engine Room

If sailing vessels move by wind power, what happens when there isn't a breeze? Find out how mariners travel the seas through the harnessing of steam and fuel to create engine power. View engines, big and small, turn over the full-sized steam engine on display, and witness power in action.

Model Mania

The creation of ship models requires skilled hands, combined with an incredible attention to detail and an in-depth knowledge of vessels. The Maritime Museum of BC has an outstanding collection of models stretching back to the HMS Nile, built in 1810 by prisoners of war, and up to 20th-century war ships and detailed builder's models for passenger vessels. Whether amateur or professionally built, it is marvellous to see the hours of dedication that went into the construction of each model.

Coastal Steam Ships

For many people living on the Pacific Coast, the Canadian Pacific Railroad (CPR) ships were a welcome sight. These comfortable, and often luxurious, coastal steamers provided an essential link between communities in Canada and the United States. Some of these vessels, such as the Princess Marguerite, are still fondly remembered today.

The Empresses

Relive the romantic era of sea travel aboard the famous Canadian Pacific Empress fleet. The names of the ships themselves symbolized luxury and comfort. For decades, these storied ships linked Canada to the world, crisscrossing the Pacific Ocean to far flung lands. There is much to take in, from fabulous models of the ships themselves to period souvenirs, and even some of the silverware used to serve lucky passengers in an era now long gone.

BC Ferries

BC Ferries operates one of the largest passenger fleets in the world. It provides an essential link and lifeline for communities all along the Pacific Coast. Often unheralded, these marine highways operate a daily service, transporting essential supplies, people, cars and trucks. The impact that BC Ferries has on the economic and cultural wellbeing of much of British Columbia is immeasurable. Check out the fabulous model of the most recent 'Spirit Class' ferries that are capable of carrying 470 cars and 2,100 passengers on each voyage.

Coast Guard

The Canadian Coast Guard's name implies protection, but this is only one aspect of this multi-faceted organization. In addition to tending to coastal security concerns, they take responsibility for such diverse functions as Air Sea Rescue, maintaining navigation aids such as buoys, and operating lighthouses. Take the time to explore the compelling stories of lighthouse operations and to view the magnificent examples of the brilliant prismatic (Fresnel) lenses that once alerted mariners to navigational hazards.

Classic Boats and Swiftsure

Why is it that whenever pleasure boaters get together, they come up with new and enjoyable ways to compete against each other? Discover the fascinating legacy of yachting as illustrated by the two popular annual Victoria boating events: the Swiftsure International Yacht Race and the Classic Boat Festival. Check out dramatic images of the Swiftsure boats in full sail and marvel at the lovingly-restored vintage vessels.

Royal Navy

The British Royal Navy's presence on the Pacific Coast goes back to the founding of Fort Victoria in the 1840s and continued right up until 1910. The legacy of the British ships and crew lives on today in numerous street, town and waterway names throughout the coastal region. Over the years, the Royal Navy built a massive naval complex in Esquimalt, complete with a graving or dry dock that allowed ships to be repaired locally and not be forced to make the lengthy journey back to England. Take the opportunity to explore the detailed model of the Esquimalt Graving Dock and see if you can figure out how this novel piece of engineering worked.

Royal Canadian Navy

When did Canada get its own navy and what was the name of the first ship to serve in the Pacific? Well, a hint is 1910 and another is the HMCS Rainbow, but that's only the beginning of your exploration of Canada's rich naval history. The Royal Canadian Navy has a proud past and present, with ships and crews bravely serving through world wars and into the age of modern global conflict. There are many highlights in this gallery, but perhaps the most significant are the exhibits telling the poignant and heroic stories of Canadians who served in the navy during the brutal war years.

Library

Did you know that the Maritime Museum has an extensive collection of nautical publications and is the proud holder of a huge quantity of original ship plans, charts, photographs and archival material? Got a puzzling marine question or have a research project on your mind? Knowledgeable volunteer staff members are on hand during the weekday afternoons to assist and encourage.

Courtroom

If this room could tell its own story, it would weave a fantastic tale of dramatic legal events and legendary personalities. Once presided over by the notorious Judge Sir Matthew Baillie Begbie in the late 19th century, this courtroom once served as both the Supreme Court of BC and the Vice-Admiralty Court for maritime legal matters. Today, the room has been restored to its former glory and offers the visitor the unique opportunity to explore one of the few remaining historic courtrooms in the country.

The museum also runs Special Exhibits that are displayed on a temporary basis. The Maritime Museum is open daily at 9:30am. Closed on Christmas Day.

Contact Details:

Maritime Museum of British Columbia

28 Bastion Square

Victoria, BC

V8W 1H9

Tel: 250-385-4222

Fax: 250-382-2869

Website: Maritime Museum of British Columbia

Royal British Columbia Museum

The Royal British Columbia Museum is a place of discovery. Through three unique galleries, the Museum showcases the human and natural history of British Columbia, and features periodic exhibitions of international renown.

Highly realistic and inviting displays, such as the Ice Age and Coastal Forest dioramas, provide visitors with a sense of having truly experienced the authentic settings of many exhibits.

Travel through the last Ice Age and emerge into British Columbian ecosystems as they exist today. The Natural History Gallery is a fascinating re-creation of our coastal forests and marine environment. You can even visit a live tidal pool for an introduction to sea anemones and starfish! The fascinating and exciting Open Ocean exhibit re-creates a submarine voyage to the depths of the marine world.

The history of British Columbia's First Nations is rich and diverse. Stories of triumph, tragedy and survival are told through a collection of remarkable artifacts, including a ceremonial Big House and totem poles.

Step back in time…from the 1970s to the 1700s. The Modern History Gallery re-creates the growth of British Columbia's industrial society through a realistic setting. Start with a stroll down a cobbled street. Experience the larger-than-life films at the National Geographic Imax Theatre, located in the Royal B.C. Museum building.

Operated by the Friends of the Royal BC Museum, the Royal Museum Shop and the National Geographic Shop carry quality items that reflect the human and national history of British Columbia. Featuring jewellery, art, publications, calendars, videos, gourmet BC food products and children's items.

Hours of Operation:
Museum: Monday to Sunday 10:00am to 5:00pm (Lobby opens at 9:45am)
IMAX: Monday to Sunday 10:00am to 8:00pm
Closed Christmas Day and New Years Day.

Contact Details:

Royal BC Museum

675 Belleville Street

Victoria, BC

V8W 9W2

Tel: 250-356-7226

Fax: 250-387-5674

Website: Royal British Columbia Museum

The Royal British Columbia Museum is located on the Inner Harbour of Victoria on Vancouver Island, opposite The Empress Hotel and the BC Legislative Buildings.

Petroglyphs

Rock carvings and paintings are found throughout the inhabited world. In British Columbia alone, over 500 examples of this type of archaeological site have been recorded, more than in any other province in Canada.

The rock carvings, or petroglyphs, were made by the aboriginal people of the region by pecking and abrading selected rock surfaces with stone tools.

The paintings, or pictographs, were applied to rock with brushes, sticks or fingers. Pigments were usually made from powdered minerals (ochres); haematite and limonite.

A binder of animal fat or fish eggs may have been added to make them adhere to the rock surface. The bonding ability and composition of the pigment is such that it easily outlasts the commercial paints of today. Over 90 per cent of all rock paintings are red.

Locations for rock art carvings and paintings were carefully chosen. They were places of power or mystery; places where the forces of nature were believed to be especially strong. They are marked by unusual natural features such as waterfalls, rock formations or caves. Nearly all sites are near water and may also be near old village sites or along trails or ancient trade routes.

For reasons not fully understood, a great many petroglyphs were carved on intertidal beach boulders submerged by the sea, or hidden below flooding rivers, appearing only when the tide is out or when the river water levels drop. Pictographs are almost always found safe and dry above the high-water mark of rivers, lakes or inlets. They were usually made on smooth, light-coloured rock surfaces where the red pigment could be easily seen.

Petroglyphs and pictographs are the records of a people with no written language and are rare links with the past native cultures of the province. They record coming of age ceremonies, performed by youths, and were burial markers or guardians for the dead. They commemorate potlatches and semi-secret events occurring during the winter ceremonials. Some, like the intertidal carvings of the coast, may have 'called' the fish into the rivers to be caught. Others marked the boundaries of hunting and fishing territories. Certain sites may have been part of secretive shamanistic rituals. A few were records of disaster: floods, landslides, storms, and wars. Many appear to have been the personal records of individuals' experiences. Although in a few cases there are ethnographic explanations of why a particular carving or painting was made, the majority are still unexplained.

The age of very few petroglyphs and pictographs is known and they are among the most recent. The stories of old people or the subject matter of some of the designs, for example historic sailing ships or horsemen, are often the only clues to age.

Of the 300 or so sites on the BC coast, fewer than 30 can be dated and most of these are approximate estimates at best. A few designs were made as late as the 1920's, but no one knows how old the older ones are.

We don't even know which are the older ones. The practice of making petroglyphs and pictographs is probably as old as man in BC. The first of the Indian people arrived in the province shortly after the ice of the last glacial age had begun to retreat some 14,000 years ago.

The earliest archaeological remains in BC, known at present, are between 9,000 12,000 years old.

It is, however, extremely unlikely that any existing petroglyphs or pictographs are that ancient since the natural forces of erosion: washing tides, abrading sand and gravel, wind, sun, rain, frost and vegetative growth, would have obliterated any early designs long ago. Field researchers often find vestiges of carvings and faint traces of paints too weathered to be recorded. The carbon 14 technique and other useful dating tools of the archaeologist can only rarely be applied to rock art sites. Estimates of the probable age of existing BC rock art range up to a maximum of 3,000 years.

Researchers are attempting to record and understand rock art before the relentless forces of erosion succeed in destroying the sites completely. Only when we understand how these carvings and paintings were made can we begin to make recommendations for their preservation. Given time, techniques can be developed to cope with natural erosion. Human damage poses a far greater threat to rock art sites. Unlike natural erosion it is unusually swift and violent. Many sites have already been lost to construction and vandalism. A site that has survived several hundred years to natural erosion can be severely damaged or totally destroyed in a few seconds by souvenir hunters chipping away at fragile surfaces, by thoughtless individuals who scratch, chalk or paint over the designs, or by the construction bulldozer.

All rock art sites in BC are protected by law. However, none can be considered as protected unless everyone recognizes them as vulnerable and respects them as a unique part of the cultural heritage of British Columbia.

Popular Petroglyph sites on Vancouver Island

Nanaimo, Vancouver Island
Petroglyph Provincial Park in Nanaimo provides the most concentrated and easily accessible collection of carvings in BC. Visitors can make their own petroglyph rubbings here, or at the Nanaimo Museum, where further information is provided on other petroglyphs in the area.

Port Alberni, Vancouver Island
One of the finest panels of petroglyphs to be seen in British Columbia is located on Sproat Lake, at the east end of Sproat Lake Provincial

Park. Located west of Port Alberni, the park combines a visit to the petroglyphs with great recreation provided on Sproat Lake.

Sooke, Vancouver Island

East Sooke Regional Park in yields magnificent Coast Salish petroglyphs at Alldridge point, designated as a provincial heritage site in 1927. Here you'll see petroglyphs carved in a style particular to the Strait of Juan de Fuca region.

Popular Petroglyph sites on the Gulf and Discovery Islands

Quadra Island, Discovoery Islands

Petroglyphs abound along the beaches of Quadra Island, around Cape Mudge Lighthouse and at the Nuyumbalees Cultural Center (formerly Kwagiulth Museum and Cultural Center) in Cape Mudge Village. "Cup and Ring" carvings on Quadra Island are identical to those found throughout Britain and Ireland, particularly in Northeastern England, and are estimated to date from the same era over 5,000 years ago. The petroglyphs in the grounds of the museum were relocated from Cape Mudge beaches for their protection.

Gabriola Island, Gulf Islands

Known as Petroglyph Island, nearly 100 petroglyphs are dotted all over Gabriola Island, accessible by a short ferry ride from Nanaimo.

The Gabriola Museum, located a short walk from the ferry dock, displays concrete replicas of a selection of the island's stone carvings, allowing visitors to take rubbings of these mythical creatures (see photo on the right).

For more information about petroglyphs and pictographs contact the Royal British Columbia Museum in Victoria

Totem Poles around Vancouver Island

Totem poles are wonderful examples of aboriginal art the ancient practice of totem carving has been handed down through generations as a way of preserving the history of local native heritage as well as honouring tribal rituals and sacred spirits of people.

There are many ways to experience the rich culture and native heritage of British Columbia's most fascinating people. There are annual powwows and a multitude of First Nations cultural journeys in every corner of the province.

The aboriginal peoples of B.C. have maintained their diverse cultures by breathing life into ancient traditions and customs and welcome all of us to experience it. For your own exploration of some of the best totem poles and aboriginal art in British Columbia here are a few areas worth visiting.

Vancouver Island and the Gulf and Discovery Islands

Alert Bay: The U'mista Cultural Centre at Alert Bay houses one of the finest collections of historical artifacts and elaborately carved masks depicting the Potlatch Ceremony of the Kwakwaka'wakw people. Alert Bay lies cradled in the arms of Cormorant Island, easily accessible by a scenic ferry ride from Port McNeill on Vancouver Island.

The Dominion Government outlawed the ceremony of the Potlatch in 1884 and authorities began to seize ceremonial regalia, including masks, rattles, robes and coppers. These ceremonies, which mark important occasions such as births, marriages, deaths or the transfer of names, were forced underground following this ruling. After more than 65 years, the confiscated items were returned from museums and private collections throughout North America.

Located on the northern end of Cormorant Island, on the outskirts of the Nimpkish Reserve at Alert Bay, stands the world's tallest totem pole at a height of 52.7 metres (173 feet) the totem is comprised of two parts. Unlike most totem poles, which are specific to a particular family, the thirteen figures depicted on this pole represent many of the tribes of the Kwakwaka'wakw nation. A collection of memorial poles may be viewed from the roadway at the Namgis Burial Grounds at Alert Bay.

Follow Highway 19 south to Campbell River. The rich native heritage of Campbell River is proudly displayed in the Campbell River Museum, which features a fine display of contemporary native masks and ceremonial items. Totem poles can be viewed at various sites throughout Campbell River: Tyee Plaza Shopping Centre, Foreshore Park, Coast Discovery Inn and Discovery Harbour Centre.

Quadra Island: A ten-minute ferry ride from Campbell River is well worth a visit. The Nuyumbalees Cultural Center (formerly Kwagiulth Museum) at Cape Mudge, on Quadra Island, displays an impressive collection of masks, potlatch regalia, rattles, whistles and other ceremonial objects associated with winter dances. These are some of the items that have filtered back from private collections over the years, after the Government of Canada first outlawed the ceremony in the early part of the 20th century.

Tofino: The Eagle Aerie Gallery located in Tofino displays interior totem poles and works of art by renowned artist Roy Vickers.

Duncan: Native history and culture are apparent throughout Duncan, the "City of Totems." A short stroll south from the museum, there are 41 intriguing totem poles to see on the self-guided walking tour just follow the yellow footprints on Duncan's sidewalks, which provide a path through the sites and the fascinating world of totem poles. The

Quw'utsun' Cultural and Conference Centre, in downtown Duncan, recreates the history and traditions of the coastal people in its buildings, displays and excellent presentations. Under the roof of a large carving shed, totem poles take shape; visitors may view work in progress.

Victoria: The Royal British Columbia Museum located in the inner harbour area of Victoria, presents a premier collection of native artifacts. Outside the museum, protected from the elements, stand some of the oldest totem poles and greet figures ever collected and preserved.

Totem poles carved in the styles of aboriginal people throughout British Columbia can be seen in Thunderbird Park, adjacent to the Royal British Columbia Museum.

In 1956, renowned Kwakwaka'wakw artist Mungo Martin and his team raised the world's tallest free-standing totem pole at 38.8 metre (128 foot) located in Beacon Hill Park, Victoria.

Sunshine Coast

Sechelt: Twelve Coast Salish totems look out over Trail Bay, at Sechelt on the Sunshine Coast. These totem poles recount the history of the Sechelt Nation, the first band in Canada to achieve self-government.

Wineries

Wineries & Wine Tours on Vancouver Island and Gulf Islands

British Columbia is fast becoming the California of the north in its production of exceptional wines. There are three regions in the province where oenophiles can find their appetites sated, and the rest of us can sip some excellent vintages at decent prices. Getting from winery to winery couldn't be easier, just follow the burgundy and white "Wine Route" signs.

Most wineries invite visitors for wine tastings and tours. Some even serve delicious food to complement their wine. As you tour, you may view the entire process, from crushing to bottling, each winery uniquely different. Where better to sample and select your favourite wine than the winery itself. Be sure to take a bottle of the region's finest when you leave.

Throughout the world, wine producing countries have set standards by which to judge their products and recognize the best. The VQA put British Columbian wines to the test of meeting premium-quality standards. This seal is awarded to British Columbia's superior wines, and is an assurance to the consumer of a certain standard in wine excellence.

MooBerry Winery on Morningstar Farm produces a wide variety of high-quality fruit wines handcrafted on Vancouver Island. Winemaker Phil Charlebois keeps busy creating new batches of flavourful wines and invites you to come by for tastings and tours. Located on a working dairy farm, there's lots to do, see and taste! Open daily from 9am to 5.

We invite you to discover B.C.'s fastest growing Wine Country. Enjoy our wineries and cideries, taste the latest vintage, picnic in a vineyard or orchard all with a backdrop of verdant hills and scenic landscapes.

The Saanich Peninsula lies just a few minutes north of Victoria. Considered Vancouver Island's latest viticultural hot spot, the Saanich Peninsula boasts the Island's only certified-organic vineyard. Your next wine tour starts in the Cowichan Valley which is reached via the Trans Canada Highway or if the prospect of negotiating the steep Malahat Drive is daunting, B.C. Ferries operates a regularly scheduled service from Brentwood Bay to Mill Bay.

The wine tour starts in the Cowichan Valley which is reached via the Trans Canada Highway or if the prospect of negotiating the steep Malahat Drive is daunting, B.C. Ferries operates a regularly scheduled service from Brentwood Bay to Mill Bay.

Your Cowichan Valley wine tour is your opportunity to sample something truly special! The Vancouver Island wine route begins at Mill Bay, at the Merridale Ciderworks, and then heads north to Cowichan Bay / Cobble Hill and the Cherry Point Vineyards. Cherry Point offers guided tours three times a day that provide an in-depth look at grape growing and wine making at a "farm" winery. Next stop is Venturi-Schulze Vineyards and the nearby Blue Grouse Vineyards. Follow the Wine Route markers, it is a fifteen-minute drive north to the southern end of the city of Duncanand Echo Valley Vineyards, Godfrey Brownell Vineyards and Zanatta Winery. Just north of the city is Alderlea Vineyards.

A half-hour drive north to Nanaimo is the Chateau Wolff Vineyard, and farther north in Port Alberni is the Chase Warren Estate Winery, the first winery in Port Alberni and the northernmost tip of the Island's wine growing region. While the vineyards, wineries, breweries, and distilleries in the Central and North Central Island regions are less concentrated than in other areas of the islands, the passion is just as strong and you'll find many of the shops and restaurants proudly offering fine locally crafted vintages, brews, and distilled spirits.

Between Parksville and Qualicum Beach in the shadow of Mt. Arrowsmith is Morningstar Farm, home to MooBerry Winery and Little

Qualicum Cheeseworks. MooBerry Winery produces a wide variety of high-quality fruit wines. Winemaker Phil Charlebois keeps busy creating new batches of flavourful wines and invites you to come by for tastings and tours. Located on a working dairy farm, there's lots to do, see and taste! Open daily from 9am to 5.

No two vineyards are alike; each has its own special favourites, as popular as Chardonnay or as rare as Agria. The region also boasts near-perfect conditions for growing premium quality cider apples. The Cowichan Valley mirrors the climate and soil conditions of the famous cider-growing regions of England and France.

The BC Gulf Islands

Located in the lee of Vancouver Island, between the island and the mainland of British Columbia, are the Gulf Islands, and their near Mediterranean climate. The Gulf Islands are currently home to 12 vineyards, many Gulf Island wineries supplement their production with grapes grown in the Okanagan Valley. Each of the Gulf Islands seems to be a world unto itself; travelling between the Southern Gulf Islands and Northern Gulf Islands can be accomplished in small hops each island deserves at least a day or two for exploring.

On Saturna Island are the Saturna Island Vineyards, the only island vineyard and winery in Canada with a resort and restaurant facilities.

On Saltspring Island, be sure to visit Salt Spring Vinyeards and Garry Oaks Winery, located between Ganges and Fulford Harbour. To the northwest of Saturna Island is Thetis Island, location of Thetis Island Vineyards. Visit Morning Bay Vineyards on North Pender Island, Gabriola Island Winery and Hornby Island on the east coast of Vancouver Island is home to three wineries. Gulf Islands ferries have a few sailings each day, so plan ahead. Diehard wine trekkers will want to hit all the wineries scattered about the islands; your best bet is to bring a bike and a tent for some serious Island Hopping.

Fishing & Guides

Vancouver Island British Columbia is famous for freshwater and saltwater fishing. Sport fishing the lakes and rivers for Pacific salmon, steelhead and trout is only surpassed by saltwater flyfishing and bottom fishing for halibut from the west coast of Vancouver Island. The luxury sportfishing resorts and and fishing lodges on Vancouver Island, the BC coast, and the many islands in the province draw anglers from around the world.

BC Sport Fishing Guide and Canadian Tide Tables
The BC Sport Fishing Guide by Fisheries and Oceans Canada provides all the information required for fishing in the province, fishing regulations, getting a fishing licence, licence fees and regulations, in-

season fishing decisions, unlawful practices, packaging of fish for transport, and reporting of fishing violations. For fishing updates by phone, call the 24-hour phone line to get red tide and sanitary closure updates, fishery openings and closures, and other info for your area: 1-866-431-3474 or 604-666-2828. Canadian Tide Tables are also available from Fisheries and Oceans Canada.

Freshwater Fishing

There are so many fishable lakes in British Columbia that even if you managed to try a different one each day of the year, you would have to start young and have a very long life (and maybe a floatplane) to visit them all. Hundreds of pleasant lakes are easily reached and fished with just a vehicle with good ground clearance, a car-top or inflatable boat or float tube, and the right fishing tackle.

Catch-and-release with a single barbless hook has become the official operative byword for those anglers fishing ocean-bound streams and rivers in BC. Attitude means a lot in fishing. Remember that the essence of sport angling is to try to hook a fish on the most sporting terms you can handle, from light tackle with artificial lures, barbless hooks, and delicate leaders to a belief that a trout is much more valuable as a living challenge to your skill than as part of a meal.

Saltwater Fishing

Salmon are the sportfish of choice in BC's marine waters. Depending on the time of year, you'll find chinook (also called king or spring salmon, or tyee if over 30 pounds/13.5 kg), coho (also called silver, blueback, or northern salmon), sockeye, or pink (also called humpy salmon). Coho aren't the biggest salmon, but they are the most sought after, as they jump and fight like trout. Sockeye are the tastiest salmon of all, while Pinks are similar in size but not as tasty.

It's a mystery, but fish oceangoing and freshwater alike are hungriest just as a slack tide is beginning to fall, and for an hour thereafter. Another well-considered tip is that the best time to fish in ocean waters is an hour before and after both high and low tides. That's just some of the fishing lore that you'll encounter when tossing a line in BC waters.

Golf & Golf Vacations

British Columbia is a golfer's paradise, with snowcapped mountains, a coastline sculpted by the Pacific rainforests, sparkling lakes, rushing rivers and lush valleys. The diversity of the province ensures some of the most scenic and challenging golf courses in North America. There are now over 250 golf courses in British Columbia. On Vancouver Island and the Gulf Islands, and along the southwest coast of the BC mainland, the climate is often perfect for golf at least eight to nine months of the year.

Arbutus Ridge Golf Club

Arbutus Ridge Golf Club is located in the seaside community of Cobble Hill on Vancouver Island, a scenic 40-minute drive from Victoria and Nanaimo and just 10 minutes away from the cultural city of Duncan. Arbutus Ridge is rated the #1 Destination Golf Course in British Columbia and the legendary 17th hole is ranked One of the Top 18 Golf Holes on Vancouver Island.

Salt Spring Island Golf & Country Club

Salt Spring Island Golf & Country Club is located on beautiful Salt Spring Island in the BC Gulf Islands, and welcomes the general public. Tee times are required 7 days a week, and times can be booked 7 days in advance by contacting the pro shop or booking online. The practice range is open daily, and clubs and power carts can be rented. Golf year round on Salt Spring winter Hours from 9am to 9pm. The Practice Range is open to all!

BC Golf Vacations

Luxury and budget golfing packages to all the top golf regions in British Columbia and Alberta, including Victoria on Vancouver Island, Whistler, Vancouver, Kamloops in High Country (BC Interior), Kelowna,

Vernon, the Okanagan, Shuswap, BC Rockies, and Banff and Jasper in Alberta. No matter what your taste or budget, we have the right accommodation and golf vacation for you. If fresh or saltwater sportfishing is your passion, we also have combined golf and fishing packages offered in Victoria. This summer don't just go golfing, go on a BC Golf Vacation!

Kayaking & Canoeing Adventures

Vancouver Island's vast number of lakes, rivers and ocean inlets are amazing to explore by canoe or kayak. Kayakers glide through BC marine parks into scenic bays and lagoons and go ashore on secluded sandy beaches and uninhabited islands. The large, relatively isolated lakes of the north and central portion of Vancouver Island are enclaves of solitude. Popular sea kayaking destinations are the Broken Group Islands in Barkley Sound (southwest coast), Broughton Archipelago off Port McNeill on the North Island, the Southern Gulf Islands off the southeast tip of the island, the Discovery Islands off Campbell River, and Desolation Sound, which is acessed from Quadra and Cortes Island, or from the BC Sunshine Coast. The kayaking season in British Columbia is from mid-May to September.

Whale Watching

Whale watching around Vancouver Island in British Columbia is an exceptional experience that will leave you awestruck after watching whales that weigh thousands of pounds frolic in their natural habitat. Killer whales (Orcas), Gray whales, Humpback whales and Minke whales ply the waves and perform their watery rituals. Whale Watching tours are operated along the east coast of Vancouver Island, from Victoria to Campbell River and Port Hardy, on the west coast of the island out of Tofino and Ucluelet, and from the BC Gulf Islands and Discovery Islands. Whalewatching at its best!

Orcas (Killer Whales) B.C's killer whale population is divided into 2 distinct groups which, curiously, never mingle. Residents travel in large pods within predictable ranges and feed primarily on fish. Transients roam in smaller groups over large areas of the coast, feeding on marine mammals such as seals, sea lions and other whales. The resident orca population is divided into 2 communities, each with its own geographical range. The ocean around Victoria is home to the southern resident community of 3 pods totalling approximately 90 magnificent animals. The northern residents total 217 whales in 16 pods, which patrol the Johnstone Strait and the waters of northern Vancouver Island and the mainland coast. The transient killer whales comprise 30 small pods of about 160 whales, and travel much farther than the resident pods. The best viewing time is from May to October.

Pacific Gray Whales migrate north along the west coast of Vancouver Island during March and April. They are easily accessible by boat, or can be viewed from mounted telescopes in the Long Beach area. Over 20,000 Gray whales participate in the longest migration of any animal, some stop to feed and rest in our protected bays, while 40 to 50 grays will spend their summers feeding off Vancouver Island.

Humpback Whales will thrill you to the north of Vancouver Island, at the outer edges of the Inside Passage, with their acrobatic behaviour and elaborate underwater song. Treasure lifetime memories of these magnificent whales breaching within metres of your boat.

Minke whales, Pacific White-sided dolphins, Harbour porpoises, Dall's porpoises, Harbour seals and Steller's sea lions are also viewed in the waters around Vancouver Island.

Nearby Regions & Towns
Parksville
Bordered by ocean and sheltered by mountains, Parksville boasts one of the finest climates in Canada, and is favoured as one of the most

popular summer family vacations destinations of Vancouver Island and British Columbia. Mild winters allow the leisurely exploration of tidal sand flats, coastal wildlife viewing, and invigorating golf year-round. Parksville was established in 1910, when the E & N Railroad first stopped at McBride Junction, as it was then known. The town was named in honour of Nelson Parks, its first settler and first postmaster.

Highway 19 (Island Highway) runs besides the open water of the Strait of Georgia on the east coast of Vancouver Island, from Parksville in the south, through the Comox Valley, and north to Campbell River and Port Hardy. Take your time as you meander through this laid-back region. Its rhythms are subtle, but with gentle probing they reveal themselves, showing greater complexity than first meets the eye. Six BC provincial parks are located within thirty minutes drive from Parksville, providing every recreational activity imaginable.

Fishing and Forestry are the traditional mainstays of the local economy, although they have both been surpassed by tourism during the last decade. The waterfront strip between Parksville and Qualicum Beach to the north is an almost continuous strip of resort development and tourism facilities.

Like its close neighbour Qualicum Beach, Parksville is an enchanting seaside village that will capture your heart. Discover for yourself why so many people return again and again to this central Vancouver Island getaway. The central location of Parksville makes this oceanside playground a convenient base from which to enjoy all your vacation activities on Vancouver Island.

Population: 11,277

Location: Parksville is located in Oceanside on the sheltered eastern shore of Vancouver Island, 7.5 miles (12 km) south of Qualicum Beach, just 37 km (23 miles) north of Nanaimo on Highway 19, and 150 km (92 miles) north of Victoria.

The Oceanside Route (Hwy 19A), is an especially scenic section of the Island Highway system that runs parallel to the Inland Island Highway (Hwy 19). The Oceanside Route follows the coastline from the Nanoose Bay area all the way to Campbell River. Enjoy the sights of Parksville and Qualicum Beach and the Lighthouse Country communities of Qualicum Bay, Bowser and Deep Bay. Continue through the charming communities of Fanny Bay, Buckley Bay, and Union Bay, and continue north through Merville, Black Creek, and Oyster River to Campbell River. Parks, beaches, golf courses, and dozens of attractions are located along the Oceanside Route, making it one of the island's most popular driving tours.

Heritage buildings from the Parksville area can be viewed at Craig Heritage Park, Museum & Archives. Among them are the French Creek Post Office (1886), the Duncan McMillan log house (1885), and the Knox Heritage Church (1912). The Museum contains exhibits related to the lives and activities of early settlers, residents, organizations and businesses in Parksville, Errington, Coombs, Hilliers, French Creek and Nanoose Bay. The park is located at the junction of Highway 19A and Franklin Gull Road, adjacent to the Visitor Centre.

The Parksville Community Park is located on Corfield Road in scenic Parksville Bay, offering a variety of activities, including the Lion's Venture Land playground, a must for younger members of the family to visit. Tennis courts, ball parks, a lacrosse box, skateboard and BMX park, covered picnic area, large field for kite flying, arena and a Community Hall are also located in the park. The beach itself offers a beautiful view, as well as swimming and sandcastle building.

Paradise Fun Park provides a profusion of colour from over 5,000 flowers, cascading waterfalls, fountains, and finely crafted fantasy scenes. Two miniature golf courses feature a full rigged pirate galleon, treasure cave, 45-foot old woman's shoe, watermill, lighthouse, Victorian Mansion, and village church.

St. Anne's Anglican Church is one of the oldest churches on Vancouver Island, built in 1894 by 45 farmers who used oxen to haul the logs to the site. To find the church, turn left off the Island Highway onto Pym Road, right onto Humphrey Road, and right onto Church Road.

Arts and Crafts abound in the area, which is home to painters, weavers, sculptors, carvers, glass blowers, and other artisans who welcome visitors to their studios. The Station Gallery at the Parksville Train Station features the work of the Arrowsmith Potters Guild, and the People's Gallery in downtown Parksville is home to exhibits presented by the Oceanside Community Arts Council. Pick up a brochure and map of the local galleries that are open to the public for tours and visits, available from the Visitor Centre.

The annual Brant Wildlife Festival celebrates the migration of up to 20,000 Black Brant geese from California and Mexico to their breeding grounds in Alaska. The beaches around Parksville and neighbouring Qualicum Beach have been the site of an annual migration of tens of thousands of brant geese since well before the settlement of the towns. With the establishment of the Brant Goose Feeding Area by the Mid Island Wildlife Watch Society, the arrival of the geese triggers annual festivities in mid April. By then, thousands of the black-hued, duck-size sea geese touch down on the beaches and marshlands surrounding Parksville and Qualicum to rest and feed on the algae, eel grasses, seaweeds, and especially herring roe. Most of the migrating birds are travelling to the Yukon-Kuskokwim delta of western Alaska, arriving at their Arctic breeding grounds in early May. Guided tours of the feeding areas take visitors to special viewing locations, or you can simply walk out on the beach with a pair of binoculars and stalk them (and the more than 200 other bird species passing through at the same time).

Beaches: If you like the beach, you'll love Parksville. With its long sandy beaches and eastern exposure, Parksville is an ideal spot to spend a few days, or the whole summer, basking in the sun and swimming in warm waters. Parksville Community Park offers great lengths of public beach on the town shoreline. Pick a location that appeals to you, park in one of the many access points, and stroll out onto the hard-packed sand. When the tide goes out in Parksville, it leaves hundreds of metres of firm golden sand, internationally acclaimed as the best building material for sandcastles!

The Parksville Beach Festival in August is the venue for the Canadian Open Sand Sculpting Competition, which draws tens of thousands of annual visitors to view a jaw-dropping array of alternately whimsical, complicated and flat-out stunning creations. The sculptures are created in early August and remain standing until the end of August.

The shores of Rhododendron Lake are lined with a stunning profusion of pink rhododendrons every spring, in late May or early June. Growing wild, these beautiful Pacific Rhododendrons (*Rhododendron macrophyllum*) are believed by botanists to belong to a strain that survived the last Ice Age. Located on forest land, access to Rhododendron Lake and the 2-hectare (5-acre) grove is by private logging road. Check for signs posted at the entrance to Northwest Bay Logging Division, approximately 7.2 km south of Parksville.

Windsurfers and Kayakers are enticed by accessible shorelines and good weather. Local outfitters will provide you with everything you need, including lessons. The federal dock at French Creek, on Hwy 19 north of Parksville, is sheltered by a sturdy breakwater, a hint that conditions do get breezy here on occasion, most notably in winter months, when winds blow from the southeast. When conditions are favourable, this is a good place to launch your kayak.

Golf: Golfers can tee off on any of the 6 exceptional and scenic golf courses in the Parksville area. Located in the Parksville area are the Morningstar Golf Club and the Fairwinds Golf and Country Club in nearby Nanoose Bay. Kids and adults love the two fun-filled 18-hole mini-golf courses located near the beach. Vancouver Island Golf Vacations.

Boat Launch sites in the area are located at Beachcomber Marina and Schooner Cove Resort in Nanoose Bay, and a public boat launch is provided at French Creek Marina, on the Island Highway between Parksville and Qualicum Beach.

Marinas: There are marinas with moorage available in French Creek, Deep Bay, and Schooner Cove. All three welcome visiting boaters, with full services nearby, including restaurants.

Mountain Biking: Mountain bike enthusiasts enjoy the challenging trails at the Hammerfest Race Course, which mixes fast logging roads with narrow, technical singletrack 6.7 miles (11.2 km). Parksville is the site of one of the major mountain bike competitions on Vancouver Island, the annual Hammerfest mountain bike race, held at Englishman River Falls Provincial Park each May. In addition to the difficult race course, the Arrowsmith Mountain Bike Club has created the Top Bridge Mountain Bike Park on the Englishman River, where more moderate adventuring awaits. To find the park, turn west off Highway 14 at the weigh scales at Kaye Road, then turn onto Chattell Road and follow it to its end, where the fun begins.

Parksville Skateboard Park offers a challenge for skateboarders, BMX riders, and in-line skaters. Ranked among the best on Vancouver Island, the skate park is located on the waterfront behind the arena, just to the south of the public beach.

Horseback Riding: The Parksville area offers many opportunities to explore the backcountry of Vancouver Island on horseback. Outfitters in the area offer instruction as well as short trail rides and overnight excursions. From alpine meadows to wooded trails, or riding on the sandy beaches, horseback riding will give you a unique perspective of this beautiful region.

Fishing: Check out the waters off French Creek, 3 miles (5 km) north of Parksville on Hwy 19A, rumoured to be a great spot to hook the big one. Kids enthusiastically cast their lines off the dock, hoping for their own vacation story to tell. The annual fall salmon run at the mouth of French Creek, as it enters the Strait of Georgia, attracts anglers to the French Creek Marina and the public boat launch adjacent to the federal dock and Lasqueti Island ferry.

Hiking: Both the Englishman River Falls and Little Qualicum Falls Provincial Parks have rambling trails that lead beside the clear waters of the pristine Englishman River and Little Qualicum rivers. An easy walk to the waterfalls is a big part of a visit to either park. For more serious hiking, the Mount Arrowsmith Trail ascends the lower slopes of Mount Arrowsmith to the site of the old ski resort, and winds up to the 1,829-metre (6,000-foot) summit of Mt. Arrowsmith. The hike is strenuous, and do not set off without a trail map. Arrowsmith Trail is the oldest intact trail on Vancouver Island. Other Mt Arrowsmith trails include the Rousseau Trail, and the Lower Ski Area Trail. The trailhead for the Arrowsmith Trail is at the Cameron Lake picnic site.

Rathtrevor Beach Provincial Park in Parksville offers a fabulous swimming beach, and over 150 bird species. So vast is its sandy, shallow shingle, particularly at low tide, that you can spend hours beachcombing and birdwatching here beneath the wide-open sky. The waters of the Strait of Georgia warm up quickly when the tide rises over these sun-baked expanses. Seals often approach the beach, following the salmon that follow the needlefish that follow the zooplankton. Join the chain!

Rathtrevor Beach Provincial Park has acres of campsites to match its 1.3 miles (2.1 km) of beaches. If you're lucky enough to be travelling in the off-season, you'll have plenty of choice from among the numerous vehicle/tent sites. Otherwise, phone ahead for reservations, particularly on weekends. Campers enjoy hot showers and gas barbeques in covered beachside picnic shelters. So good does the living get here that some families spend their entire vacations at Rathtrevor Beach, where the maximum stay permitted is 14 consecutive days.

Englishman River Falls Provincial Park, situated along the Englishman River, features a spectacular canyon between two beautiful waterfalls cascading along the descending riverbed. This 97-hectare park offers several walking trails along the Englishman River that meander through lush old-growth forests of cedar, arbutus, fir, maple and hemlock. Gaze up among the tall timbers where fingers of sunlight slant down to the ferns below. You'll find 105 vehicle/tent sites and there's great picnicking, summer swimming, and a 2-mile walking trail that passes through a stand of maple trees to an impressive waterfall and gorge. Located south of nearby Errington.

Little Qualicum Falls Provincial Park straddles the scenic Little Qualicum River, where impressive waterfalls cascade and plummet down a rocky gorge in a beautiful forest setting. This magnificent 440-hectare park is a popular family recreation area, and is perhaps the most magnificent park on Vancouver Island. Little Qualicum Falls incorporates the entire southern shore of Cameron Lake, adjacent to MacMillan Provincial Park and the awesome Cathedral Grove

Rainforest. Rambling riverside trails and a number of cool, clear swimming holes make Little Qualicum Falls a favoured destination.

MacMillan Provincial Park is famous for Cathedral Grove, one of the most accessible stands of giant Douglas-fir trees in BC. Some of these trees are 800 years old, and walking the trails through this virgin coastal forest can be quite an inspirational experience. Loop trails on either side of the highway lead awe-struck visitors through the mighty forest stands. The south loop showcases the largest Douglas-fir trees, with the biggest one measuring over 9 metres in circumference. The trail on the northern side of the road winds through groves of ancient Western Red Cedar to the shores of Cameron Lake. The 136-hectare park is located on Highway 4 on the shores of Cameron Lake, 20 miles (31 km) west of Parksville.

Caving: There are several hundred significant caves to explore on Vancouver Island, including those at Horne Lake Caves Provincial Park, 12 miles (20 km) west of Hwy 19 near Qualicum Bay. The park protects seven caves in the Horne Lake Cave system. A small fee is charged for tours in July and August, conducted by knowledgeable guides from the Canadian Cave Conservancy, a nonprofit organization devoted to proper management, protection, and interpretation of Canada's cave resources. If you're here in summer, plan to join the challenging Karst

Trail and Riverbend Trail tours, which last about two hours. You can take a self-guided tour of Main Cave and Lower Main Cave throughout the year. Although the distance covered isn't great about 200 metres you'll have to bend, duck, and squeeze your way through a series of narrow passages.

No matter when you arrive, prepare yourself for a tour by dressing warmly, wearing sturdy boots, and carrying a bright flashlight. (Helmets and lights are provided on guided tours. For those with a lust to squeeze deeper into the cave system, the three-to-four-hour Riverbed Bottoming trip leads down through a series of vertical pits, the deepest of which is nearly 60 feet (19 metres). A gravel road leads to the parking area and trailhead at the far end of Horne Lake. A footbridge spans the Qualicum River, from where a rough limestone trail leads to the Main Cave.

The Kulth Music Fest is held in nearby Coombs in mid July. The Kulth is a festival created for people of all ages, with both local and international artists performing folk music, electronic music, and Reggae music. The festival is located at the Coombs Rodeo Grounds on the Alberni Highway.

From the town of Parksville, Highway 4 (Pacific Rim Highway) begins to wind across the spine of the Vancouver Island mountains to Port

Alberni and the open ocean at Ucluelet and Tofino, all three of which are sheltered harbours. This is the route to the Pacific Rim.

To the north of Parksville, Qualicum Beach gently spreads in front of one of the most pleasant small towns on the east side of Vancouver Island. Pause here at any of the numerous beachside pullouts and smell the salt air intermingled with the perfume from the many private and public floral displays.

South of Parksville, the waterfront community of Nanoose Bay is a hot spot for golfers, clam diggers and water sports enthusiasts. The peninsula's large, protected harbour is a destination for visiting boats from around the world, and home to an assortment of marinas, one as large as 400 berths. The Nanoose Bay area is a vacationer's paradise, offering a wealth of recreational activities. Further south is the bustling commercial centre of Nanaimo, home to the BC ferry terminals at Departure Bay and Duke Point. Once past Nanaimo, a succession of charming villages leads you into the Cowichan Valley.

Offshore to the north of Parksville lies Lasqueti Island, the first of several northern Gulf Islands that you catch glimpses of as the Island Highway heads north towards Courtenay and Campbell River. Farther off in the distance is the dark profile of Texada Island. Largely undeveloped, Lasqueti Island lies southwest of Texada Island, a short distance across the Strait of Georgia from Parksville and Qualicum Beach. The island is a quaint and eccentric little community of self-reliant homesteaders who enjoy the island's mild climate and relative isolation. Catch the ferry from French Creek, midway between Qualicum Beach and Parksville.

Circle Tours: See the best of BC when you embark upon one of the many circle tours that take in Vancouver Island, the Discovery Coast, and the Sunshine Coast. The coastal tours involve exciting road and ferry trips on BC Ferries, and scenic highways flank the coast, taking you through charming beachside communities, rolling farmlands and majestic mountain ranges. Check out the Sunshine Coast and Vancouver Island Circle Tour, and other Circle Tours in British Columbia.

Getting There: Island Highway 19 is an express route from Victoria to Port Hardy. If you like a more leisurely pace, follow the signs to the original coastal Highway 19A, the 'Oceanside Route'. Coach lines offer regularly scheduled trips north, south and west through the Oceanside area, connecting to other parts of Vancouver Island.

Most visitors arrive on Vancouver Island by ferry. From Vancouver, depart from either the Tsawwassen Terminal south of Vancouver to Duke Point or from Horseshoe Bay in West Vancouver to Departure

Bay in Nanaimo. Once on the island, head north on Highway 19, which takes you directly to Oceanside. There is a shuttle service to Parksville/Qualicum Beach for foot passengers on the Horseshoe Bay run. Buses also leave Vancouver Bus and Train Terminal for the island ferries on a regular basis, with connections to Oceanside communities through Nanaimo.

Port Alberni

Port Alberni is nestled in the Alberni Valley at the head of Alberni Inlet, the longest inlet on Vancouver Island.

For decades the main industries of Port Alberni have been mining and logging, but today the town is considered a major tourist hub, situated as it is on the fringe of the island's wilderness in surroundings that include mountains, pristine lakes, surging rivers filled with salmon and trout, and rain forests of giant trees towering more than 200 feet into the sky.

With the increased popularity of Pacific Rim National Park, Barkley Sound and Clayoquot Sound, many visitors are basing their vacations in Port Alberni, and taking trips to a variety of west coast locations.

Port Alberni was named after Captain Don Pedro de Alberni, a Spanish officer who commanded Fort San Miguel at Nootka Sound on the west coast of Vancouver Island from 1790 to 1792. Before Europeans came, the region incorporating Alberni and the West Coast of Vancouver Island was the traditional territory of the Tseshaht and Hupacasath First Nations of the Nuu-Chah-Nulth Tribal Council. The Nuu-chah-nulth were previously called the Nootka. Many place names in Port Alberni have a Nuu-chah-nulth origin, such as Somass (washing), Kitsuksis (log across mouth of creek), Pacheena (foamy), and Nootka (go around). Ancient petroglyph carvings can be found at Sproat Lake.

Port Alberni is truly the *Salmon Capital of the World*, with adjacent waters boasting all five species of Pacific salmon. Port Alberni has cemented this status by winning the first ever title of Ultimate Fishing Town as awarded in 2010 by the World Fishing Network, an American television network.

Port Alberni's harbour district is thick with tackle shops, boat rentals, and fishing charters. This is definitely one of the major hubs for angling on Vancouver Island and is the best resource centre for information on fishing locally in both saltwater and freshwater.

Visitors come to Port Alberni year round to sport fish Alberni Inlet and Barkley Sound for chinook, coho, and sockeye salmon. Salmon school in the inlet before ascending to the spawning grounds. Timing is crucial if you wish to take advantage of their presence. One day they're here; the next, they're gone, so plan ahead. In general, the Alberni Inlet and Barkley Sound offer year-round fishing. Salmon is the prize catch in these waters, but so too are halibut.

The City of Port Alberni offers a deep sea port, beautiful waterfront quays, an airport, a new hospital, shopping malls, a casino, and a well-developed array of recreational facilities. The Alberni Harbour Quay has recently been revitalized by the construction of Spirit Square and a new waterfront boardwalk. The area is a people's place, with stores and restaurants, and art galleries.

On Saturdays throughout the year there is a lovely Farmer's Market where you can find a variety of handicrafts, as well as groceries for your camping or kayaking trip. Also in the area are the Maritime Museum and a regularly scheduled cargo and passenger ship that cruises Alberni Inlet and the communities of Barkley Sound.

Port Alberni is the *Start of the Pacific Rim Experience*. Be sure and stop at the spectacular new Visitor Centre as you enter the town. To the west of Port Alberni are the communities of Ucluelet and Tofino, and the spectacular Long Beach. Port Alberni is also the starting point of a 102-km unpaved road to the village of Bamfield, and the start of the famous West Coast Trail.

Population: 18,790

Location: Port Alberni is located in the Alberni Valley on Vancouver Island, at the head of Alberni Inlet, 29 miles (47km) west of Parksville on Pacific Rim Highway 4.

Alberni Inlet: Port Alberni sits at the head of Alberni Inlet, Vancouver Island's longest inlet. The town is actually a saltwater port, situated 40 kilometres from the Pacific Ocean on the west coast of Vancouver Island! The Alberni Inlet is a long indentation that reaches so far inland from the Pacific Ocean that it comes to within just 30 miles (48 km) of Parksville on the east coast of Vancouver Island.

Alberni Valley Museum collections tell the story of Alberni Valley community history, Nuu Chah Nulth art and culture and the region's industrial roots, from logging to fishing and farming. Displays include an exceptional display of local artifacts and original native crafts, such as the intricately woven cedar bark baskets of the Nuu Chah Nulth people.

Murals: Eighteen colourful murals adorn the buildings of downtown Port Alberni, celebrating the life and heritage of the Alberni Valley. A self-guided tour map of the Port Alberni murals is available at the Visitor Centre.

Alberni Harbour Quay at the foot of Argyle Street in downtown Port Alberni is a friendly conglomeration of restaurants, galleries, tour operators, and shops where visitors can find an island souvenir for friends back home. In summer, the steam locomotive Two Spot departs from the station at the head of the quay for a tourist tour along the waterfront.

Whaling Sculpture: On display on the boardwalk at Victoria Quay is a Nuu-Chah-Nulth Whaling Canoe sculpture, carved from yellow and red cedar. The elaborate carving is a replica of an historical First Nation whaler's canoe pursuing a grey whale, considered as a great gift from the Creators.

McLean Mill National Historic Site: Step back in time and experience the heritage of British Columbia's forest industry at the restored McLean Steam Sawmill. A troupe of professional actors breathes life into the very people who built this province. Through daily interpretive drama, songs, stories, and dance, the period characters show how it was for the pioneers of the logging industry. The site is accessible to the public year round, with mill demonstrations, theatre presentations, and tours operating from May to September. Located on Smith Road off Beaver Creek Road, north of Port Alberni.

1964 Tsunami: Port Alberni was devastated by a tsunami on Good Friday, March 27, 1964. The tidal wave reached three metres above the high water mark and destroyed everything in its path without loss of life! Anchorage in Alaska was rocked by one of the strongest earthquakes of the century, measuring 8.5 on the Richter scale and raising a section of the ocean floor by 15 metres. The resulting waves travelled from the Gulf of Alaska, reaching speeds in open water of up to 720 km/h, At midnight, 4-1/2 hours after the earthquake, the first of these waves entered the mouth of Alberni Inlet. As the waves entered the funnel-shaped inlet, the narrowing shoreline forced the waves to pile up. In 10 minutes the wave advanced 60 kilometres (360 km/h) toward Port Alberni. The second wave was the most damaging, cresting three metres above the high tide mark when it raced inland and into the homes of sleeping residents. Four less forceful waves stormed in between 3am and 6.45am, reaching levels about two metres above the high tide mark. When the sun broke through the mist the next morning, 58 properties had been destroyed, 350 buildings damaged, and 300 cars written off, but nobody was drowned or even seriously injured.

Robertson Creek Hatchery officially opened in 1960, when it was the largest artificial spawning channel in North America. It is now the most successful hatchery on Vancouver Island, producing nearly 10 million smolts annually; chinook salmon, coho salmon and steelhead trout. The hatchery is open from 08:30 to 15:30 Monday to Friday, with an open house on the third Sunday of October every year. Drive through

Port Alberni on Highway 4 and turn right on Great Central Lake Road. Follow the signs to the hatchery.

Somass Estuary Project: Almost 160 species of birds have been found on the land that is part of the Somass Estuary Project. Comprised of intertidal marshes, mudflats, forested islands and lowland meadows, the estuary lies at the head of the narrow 40-km-long Alberni Inlet, creating one of the most protected winter feeding sites for waterfowl migrating and wintering along the west coast of Vancouver Island. Some of the winter residents include the once endangered Trumpeter Swan, Canada Geese, and many species of ducks. The Estuary teems with black bears, bald eagles, black-tailed deer, beavers, mink, harbour seals, as well as five species of salmon. This property was purchased by Ducks Unlimited, and a variety of other government and local organizations, to protect it from development and to protect the fish and bird habitat. The Somass River is the second largest river on Vancouver Island, draining the land around Sproat Lake, Great Central Lake and reaching into Strathcona Provincial Park.

Flying Water Tankers: During the forest fire season, the gigantic Martin Mars water bombers use Sproat Lake for their runway as they thunder off to extinguish forest fires. The largest water bombers in the world, these aircraft can scoop up to 27 tons of water off the lake surface. One or more of the enormous red and white water bombers are moored on Sproat Lake at the Coulson Flying Tankers visitor centre on Cherry Creek Road, which is open to the public daily during July and August. Guided tours of the Philippine Mars are available.

Spawning Salmon: Upwards of half a million salmon make their way to their spawning grounds via the Stamp River in the fall. Follow Beaver Creek Road about 7.5 miles (12 km) north from Hwy 4 to Stamp River Provincial Park. Watch for pullouts beside the river along the way. A spectacular waterfall at the park is perhaps the best place on Vancouver island to see salmon migrating. Below the falls is a canyon where you can view hundreds of fish awaiting their turn at the falls and the fish ladder beside it. Robertson Creek Fish Hatchery place video cameras at the top of the fish ladder for public viewing and to count the numbers of fish using it.

Fishing: Port Alberni hums with visitor activity during fishing season. The town has a freshwater fishing side that would be the envy of any fishing town anywhere. Freshwater streams and lakes near Port Alberni are filled with steelhead, rainbow, and cutthroat trout. Actively feeding spring salmon begin appearing in March as they follow the bountiful herring and anchovy spawning runs. Springs linger into May, when they are replaced by early-run tyee (also called chinook) salmon migrating in the Alberni Inlet. Sockeye salmon succeed the early-run tyee in late June and are joined by late-run tyee, the largest of all salmon, in July and August. The Somas River runs through the heart of town. Bank casting is possible from a number of locations beside Highway 4 and along Hector Road off Hwy 4 west of Port Alberni. Just north of Port Alberni, the Stamp River would probably make every chinook and steelhead angler's top ten list. A winter run of steelhead occurs in the Stamp River, beginning in January and lasting through March.

Sproat Lake also has a good reputation for rainbow trout angling, particularly June through September. Use the boat launch here to head out for some trolling or casting. April and May are good months for steelhead in Sproat Lake.

China Creek is one of the chief staging areas for fishing the Alberni Inlet, located 9 miles (14 km) south of Port Alberni on the road to Bamfield. You'll find a marina, a private campground, a boat launch, and quite possibly a salmon or two. Primary fish runs in China Creek include cutthroat trout from January to March, and steelhead from October to December. China Creek offers a privately operated marina and campground.

Golf: The Hollies Executive Golf Course is surrounded by the Beaufort Range and breathtaking views of Mount Arrowsmith. The 9-hole par 30 public course offers a fully stocked pro-shop, club rentals, snack shop and licensed lounge. Located 2 km past the Visitor Centre on Highway 4 entering Port Alberni. Open daily from dawn till dusk, with no tee times required. Vancouver Island Golf Vacations.

Camping: The private Arrowvale Campground offers 40 open and wooded sites on Hector Road, and the Ark Resort at the east end of Great Central Lake has a campground with RV and tent sites.

Houseboating: Enjoy a vacation with a difference, with all the comforts of home. Houseboating is popular on Sproat Lake, located west of Port Alberni. The warm water is great for swimming, and the boat provides a great base for freshwater fishing, waterskiing and windsurfing, and for scenic cruises to view the many beautiful homes on the lake.

Sightseeing Tours: Embark on guided day hikes, nature tours, wildlife safaris and birding excursions on Central Vancouver Island and the Pacific Rim, or sign up for a whale watching excursion down Alberni Inlet. Anglers can rise above the trees on a helicopter ride to a remote mountain lake for a day of fishing. Vancouver Island Soaring Centre gets visitors soaring effortlessly like an eagle in the sky. Gliders are towed high above the Port Alberni Airport and released for dramatic scenic flights over the Alberni Valley, soaring above magnificent mountains, forests, lakes, waterfalls and ocean inlets.

Hiking: Port Alberni has some of the best hiking on Vancouver Island. There are over 100 trails for hiking, mountain biking and horseback riding in and around the Alberni Valley. Three of the popular Port Alberni Hiking Trails are detailed below.

Log Train Trail in Log Train Regional Park in Port Alberni offers 25 km of trail for hikers, cyclists and horse riders through the beautiful Alberni Valley. The trail stretches along the foot of the Beaufort Range, leading to the McLean Mill Historic Site. The Log Train Trail was originally part of the Bainbridge Mill rail-logging operation. The trail is accessible from many points in the Alberni Valley, but the easiest start is from the trailhead sign on Highway 4.

Stamp Long River Trail provides access to 7.5 km of beautiful old growth riparian on the east bank of the Stamp River, running mostly parallel to the river. Several short switchbacks provide contrasting views of the river from above. Ancient firs and cedars can be found along the length of the trail, and there is a particularly fine stand of old growth near the north end. Eagles, hawks, mergansers, dippers and other water birds are frequently seen. In fall, bears are frequently encountered feeding on salmon. Care should be taken to avoid encountering a feeding bear. Caution should also be exercised during winter when water levels are high. The trail can be accessed from either the south or north ends, but there are no intermediate access points.

Della Falls is Canada's highest waterfall, at 1,444 feet (440 metres). Along with Mount Waddington, British Columbia's highest mountain, Della Falls is one of the most awesome and least visited natural attractions in BC. Della Falls lies within Strathcona Provincial Park, northwest of Port Alberni, and requires a hike of 3 to 5 days via the historic Drinkwater **Trail** (moderate; 20 miles/32 km return). The trailhead is at the west end of the 18-mile (29-km) long Great Central Lake.

Stamp River Provincial Park lies about 9 miles (14 km) north of Port Alberni. This park is often used by anglers who come to fish for salmon in the Stamp River, an excellent place to catch the fall salmon runs. The park features a riverside campsite and hiking trails to the scenic Stamp Falls, a beautiful waterfall that is sure to soothe even the most jangled of nerves. Take an easy drive on Beaver Creek Road north of Hwy 4 from the centre of Port Alberni.

Sproat Lake Provincial Park is a popular family camping destination 8 miles (13 km) west of Port Alberni on Hwy 4. The park overlooks an expansive body of freshwater, with Mount Anderson rising to the south. The park sits beside a sheltered bay at the northeast corner of Sproat Lake. Many of those who camp here come to take advantage of the triple boat launch and large public marina. In fact, there are twice as many boat slips as campsites. Sproat Lake Park has a fine beach and much warmer water than the ocean farther west. A distinctive historical feature in the park is the Native Indian rock carvings, known as petroglyphs.

Taylor Arm Provincial Park is a forested site on the north shore of Sproat Lake, about 15 kms west of Port Alberni on Hwy 4. The park features an astounding number of undeveloped campsites, hiking trails lead beside the lake and onto the mountain ridges above the park.

Mount Arrowsmith Regional Park offers good hiking and rock climbing, with superb views of Vancouver Island. Winter activities include cross-country skiing, snowmobiling, and ice-climbing. The trailhead for the Arrowsmith Trail is at the Cameron Lake picnic site. The trail ascends the lower slopes of the mountain to the site of the old ski resort, and winds up to the summit of Mt. Arrowsmith. The hike is strenuous, and do not set off without a trail map. Arrowsmith Trail is the oldest intact trail on Vancouver Island. Other trails include the Rousseau Trail, and the Lower Ski Area Trail.

Mount Arrowsmith Massif Regional Park encompasses the peaks of Mt Arrowsmith and Mt Cokely. Ecological significance includes the parks two key salmon producing rivers, the Englishman River and Little Qualicum River, as well as providing habitat for endangered wildlife species such as the white-tailed ptarmigan and Vancouver Island Marmot. Rising to a majestic height of 5,968 feet (1,819 metres), the Mount Arrowsmith massif dominates the skyline from both sides of Vancouver Island. Previously Crown Forest Reserve, the park was declared a regional park in November 2008 and officially opened in September 2009. Access to the mountain is located near the summit of Highway 4, 9 km east of Port Alberni.

Port Alberni Farmers' Market is held in downtown Port Alberni in the centre of Harbour Quay every Saturday morning till noon throughout the year. The traditional farmers' market promotes local produce and products, providing a wide assortment of meats, fruit and vegetables, free-range eggs, breads, soaps, arts and crafts.

Port Alberni Salmon Festival is the pinnacle of the salmon fishing culture. The popular world-class fishing derby is held in Port Alberni every year on Labour Day weekend, when anglers come from all over North America to test their fishing skills. You never know, you might just win a cash price for reeling in the biggest salmon!

Alberni District Fall Fair in September features a variety of homespun products, a midway, an art show, a 4-H competition, country fair baking, livestock competitions, and the famous Logger Sports Day. Bring the whole family to the 4-day event. Unserviced camping is available on either side of the horse rings.

Thunder in the Valley is an annual drag racing event and carshow held at the Alberni Valley Airport in August.

MV Frances Barkley: Set sail for spectacular West Coast scenery aboard the *MV Frances Barkley*, based in Port Alberni, travelling down Alberni Inlet to Barkley Sound and the coastal villages of Bamfield (year round) and Ucluelet (June to September). Sprinkled throughout Barkley Sound are the Broken Group Islands, a series of islands and shallow reefs that support a profusion of marine life. Kayaking and diving are excellent in the area. The Broken Group **Islands** provide kayakers and divers with a true West Coast experience in sheltered water.

East of Port Alberni is Parksville, an enchanting seaside village on the east coast of Vancouver Island. With its long sandy beaches and eastern exposure, Parksville is an ideal spot to spend a few days, or the whole summer, basking in the sun and swimming in warm waters.

West of Port Alberni is the Pacific Rim on the West Coast of Vancouver Island, incorporating magnificent Long Beach, the communities of Tofino and Ucluelet, and Pacific Rim National Park.

Southwest of the Alberni Valley is Bamfield, nestled quietly in a protected inlet on the south shore of Barkley Sound. This tiny fishing and harbour village, heavily populated by marine biologists, is a quiet, unassuming village where the love of the land and sea prevails.

Coombs

A popular stopping point for tourists on the way to the west coast, the little village of Coombs is dotted with several heritage buildings, small gift and craft shops and antique stores. Coombs is also known for the family of goats nimbly grazing on the grass rooftop of the Coombs Old Country Market.

Coombs was established at the turn of the twentieth century by families who arrived as part of the Salvation Army's immigration program, a humanitarian scheme that brought nearly a quarter of a million poor English and Welsh to Canada.

A handful of families settled here around 1910 under the leadership of the Salvation Army's Ensign Crego. The community was named after the Army's Canadian Commissioner, Captain Thomas Coombs.

Location: Coombs is located on the Port Alberni/Tofino Highway 4, 5.5 miles (9 km) west of Parksville on Vancouver Island.

Be sure to stop in to the Coombs General Store, which has been serving every need of the community since 1910.

The Coombs Emporium and Frontier Town will keep everyone entertained and excited.

July is the time for Old West activities at the Coombs Rodeo Ground; an old time fiddlers jamboree, a bluegrass festival, and the Annual Coombs Rodeo.

The annual Coombs Country Arts & Crafts Fair is held in mid July at the Coombs Rodeo Ground. Visitors come for the arts, crafts, concessions, entertainment, and many other exciting demonstrations.

Butterfly World and the Emerald Forest Bird Garden are popular attractions where you can stroll amongst hundreds of exotic butterflies flying free in an indoor tropical rainforest. Witness the entire life cycle of these amazing insects. Spectacular flowering plants and foliage, fascinating birds, waterfalls and streams all contribute to make this a photographer's paradise and a truly memorable experience for the entire family.

The World Parrot Refuge in Coombs provides a "home for life" for previously owned pet parrots. This educational facility is dedicated to the health and well being of parrots, and is open to the public to raise awareness of the growing problems of parrots in captivity. The refuge has created a more natural environment for the birds, with 23,000 square feet of indoor, heated, free-flight aviaries, and 16,000 square feet of easily accessed outdoor flights for the warmer months. The World Parrot Refuge is located at 2116 Alberni Highway.

Hamilton Marsh provides natural habitat for such marsh birds and is particularly active in spring and fall with migrations of ducks and geese. Woodland trails from the small parking lot lead you to and around the marsh, with a viewing platform for closer observation of marsh inhabitants. Hamilton Marsh is located approximately 4 km north of Coombs on South Hilliers Road, just off the Alberni Highway 4.

The Little Qualicum Spawning Channel on the Little Qualicum River is accessed via Melrose Road. Turn north off Highway 4, 3.5 miles (6 km) west of Coombs, and follow the signs to the hatchery. Over 4 million chinook salmon are raised annually, with the best visiting times being

February to June and October to November. This hatchery is not to be confused with the big Qualicum Falls Hatchery, located on the Qualicum River north of Horne Lake.

Golf: There are no fewer than 6 world-class golf courses in the nearby Parksville and Qualicum Bay area, and the pleasant, sunny climate means play continues year-round. Select from the *Morningstar Golf Club* in Parksville, or Arrowsmith Golf & Country Club, Eaglecrest Golf Club, Pheasant Glen Golf Resort, and Qualicum Beach Memorial Golf Course in Qualicum Beach. Golf Vacations on Vancouver Island.

Spend an afternoon lazing on the beach at the Cameron Lake Recreation Site, surrounded by mountains and forests in the Little Qualicum Falls Provincial Park on Highway 4, 7 miles (12 km) west of Coombs. Facilities at the lake include picnic sites, a boat Launch (private), and campsites (private and provincial). Cameron Lake is stocked with rainbow and cutthroat trout, and offers good fishing through summer. Anglers can test their fly fishing skills on the lake's brown trout, often the most difficult of trout to catch in B.C. Strong winds blow here in the afternoon, which attracts windsurfers but definitely deters those in small boats. Boaters and paddlers should take note of the strong and sudden gusts of wind often experienced on Cameron Lake.

At the west end of Cameron Lake is the Beaufort Picnic Site, another fine location for picnicking and swimming adjacent to the campground in the Little Qualicum Falls Provincial Park. Picnic tables are arranged beside the beach. Cameron Lake is bordered by steep mountains: Mt. Wesley to the north and Mt. Arrowsmith to the south.

Little Qualicum Falls Provincial Park straddles the scenic Little Qualicum River, where impressive waterfalls cascade and plummet down a rocky gorge in a beautiful forest setting. This magnificent 440-hectare park is a popular family recreation area, and is perhaps the most magnificent park on Vancouver Island, Little Qualicum Falls incorporates the entire southern shore of Cameron Lake, adjacent to MacMillan Provincial Park and the awesome Cathedral Grove Rainforest.

MacMillan Provincial Park is famous for Cathedral Grove, one of the most accessible stands of giant Douglas-fir trees in British Columbia. Some of these trees are 800 years old, and walking the trails through this virgin coastal forest can be quite an inspirational experience. Loop trails on either side of the highway lead awe-struck visitors through the mighty forest stands. The south loop showcases the largest Douglas-fir trees, with the biggest one measuring over 9 metres in circumference. The trail on the northern side of the road winds through groves of ancient Western Red Cedar to the shores of Cameron Lake. The 136-hectare park is located on Highway 4 on the shores of Cameron Lake, 7.5 miles (20 km) west of Coombs.

Englishman River Falls Provincial Park, situated along the Englishman River, features a spectacular canyon between two beautiful waterfalls cascading along the descending riverbed. This 97-hectare park offers several walking trails that meander through lush old-growth forests of cedar, arbutus, fir, maple and hemlock along the Englishman River. Gaze up among the tall timbers where fingers of sunlight slant down to the ferns below. You'll find vehicle/tent sites and there's great picnicking, summer swimming and a 2-mile walking trail that passes through a stand of maple trees to an impressive waterfall and gorge. Located 3.5 miles (6 km) south of nearby Errington.

Hiking: The Mount Arrowsmith area offers good hiking and rock climbing, with breathtaking views of Vancouver Island. The trailhead for the Arrowsmith Trail is at the Cameron Lake picnic site, and winds up to the 6,000-foot summit in the Mount Arrowsmith Regional Park. The hike is strenuous, and do not set off without a trail map! Evidence of a forest fire that roared through here 300 years ago is still visible on the thick bark of the tallest Douglas fir, and windstorms during the winter of 1997 toppled hundreds of trees. Located 7.5 miles (12 km) west of Coombs on the Alberni Highway 4.

Both Englishman River Falls and Little Qualicum Falls Provincial Parks have rambling trails that lead beside the clear waters of these pristine rivers. A walk to the falls is a big part of a visit to either park.

Fishing: There's excellent bank casting for rainbow and cutthroat trout on the Englishman **River**, either near the river mouth on the Strait of Georgia near Parksville or in Englishman River Falls Provincial Park. There's a steelhead run as well in the river. Unfortunately, a decline in salmon stocks in BC has forced closures on fishing for a number of species, so be sure to check in advance. Over the past century, brown trout have been successfully introduced to a number of Vancouver Island rivers, such as the Little Qualicum. The best access to the river for bank casting is at Little Qualicum Falls Provincial Park. You'll also find good trolling and boat casting in Cameron Lake, part of which also lies within the park. There's a boat launch at the picnic grounds on Cameron Lake.

The Kulth Music Fest is held in Coombs in mid July. The Kulth is a festival created for people of all ages, with both local and international artists performing folk music, electronic music, and Reggae music. The festival is located at the Coombs Rodeo Grounds on the Alberni Highway.

To the east of Coombs is the seaside resort town of Parksville. Bordered by ocean and sheltered by mountains, Parksville boasts some of the finest beaches in Canada, including those at Rathtrevor Beach Provincial Park. When the tide goes out in Parksville, it leaves hundreds of metres of firm golden sand internationally acclaimed as the best building material for sandcastles!

Directly north of Coombs is another seaside pleasureland. Steeped in a quaint British heritage, modern day Qualicum Beach offers visitors the same gentle countryside and golden, seemingly endless sandy beaches as Parksville, plus 4 top golf courses.

Errington

In the shadow of Vancouver Island's mountain spine, this tiny village was first settled by Duncan McMillan, who named this new settlement after Errington, a small village in England's Northumberland county.

Now home to an eclectic assortment of farmers, artists and craftspeople, Errington is also the gateway to the Englishman River Falls in the magnificent Englishman River Falls Provincial Park.

Location: Errington is located in the foothills of Arrowsmith Mountain on Errington Road, off Highway 4, just south of Parksville and Qualicum Beach on the east coast of central Vancouver Island.

Visit the North Island Wildlife Recovery Association, located on an 8-acre plot of land in Errington, where injured birds and mammals are nursed back to health and visitors are educated on wildlife issues. The centre is open from the March Spring break through to December, offering a beautiful park and non-releasable animals and birds such as eagles, owls, turkey vulture, falcons, hawks, and black bears. Adopt a heron, a fawn, an otter or an eagle!

Stop by the Errington Farmers Market at the Errington Hall on Errington Road, a community based market specializing in agricultural products, arts, crafts and live entertainment. Saturday mornings from 10 am to 1 pm, mid-May to mid-September.

Meet the animals at Tiger Lily Farm, a children's farm featuring a hands-on experience with typical BC farm animals, pony rides, birthday parties and more. Hug the little lambs, learn how to milk a goat, count the chickens, or bottle-feed a calf!

Golf: There are no fewer than 6 world-class golf courses in the nearby Parksville and Qualicum Bay area, and the pleasant, sunny climate means play continues year-round. Select from the Morningstar Golf

Club in Parksville, or Arrowsmith Golf & Country Club, Eaglecrest Golf Club, Pheasant Glen Golf Resort, and Qualicum Beach Memorial Golf Course in Qualicum Beach. Vancouver Island Golf Vacations.

The Little Qualicum Spawning Channel on the Little Qualicum River is accessed via Melrose Road. Turn north off Highway 4, 3.5 miles (6 km) west of Coombs, and follow the signs to the hatchery. Over 4 million chinook salmon are raised annually, with the best visiting times being February to June and October to November. This hatchery is not to be confused with the big Qualicum Falls Hatchery, located on the Qualicum River north of Horne Lake.

Englishman River Falls Provincial Park is situated along the Englishman River, featuring a spectacular canyon between two beautiful waterfalls that cascade along the descending riverbed. The 97-hectare Englishman River Falls Park offers several walking trails that meander along the Englishman River through lush old-growth forests of cedar, arbutus, fir, maple and hemlock.

Gaze up among the tall timbers where fingers of sunlight slant down to the ferns below. You'll find vehicle and tent campsites, and there's great picnicking, summer swimming, and a 2-mile walking trail that passes through a stand of maple trees to an impressive waterfall and gorge. One hiking trial in the park leads to centuries-old petroglyphs depicting a bear and two whales. Located 3.5 miles (6 km) south of Errington.

Fishing: There's excellent bank casting for rainbow and cutthroat trout on the Englishman River, either near the river mouth on the Strait of Georgia near Parksville or in Englishman River Falls Provincial Park. There's a steelhead run as well in the river. Unfortunately, a decline in salmon stocks in British Columbia has forced closures on fishing for a number of species, so be sure to check in advance. Over the past century, brown trout have been successfully introduced to a number of Vancouver Island rivers, such as the Little Qualicum. The best access to the river for bank casting is at Little Qualicum Falls Provincial Park. You'll also find good trolling and boat casting in Cameron Lake, part of which also lies within the park. There's a boat launch at the picnic grounds on Cameron Lake.

Hiking: Both Englishman River Falls and Little Qualicum Falls Provincial Parks have rambling trails that lead beside the clear waters of these pristine rivers. A walk to the falls is a big part of a visit to either park.

MacMillan Provincial Park is famous for Cathedral Grove, one of the most accessible stands of giant Douglas-fir trees in British Columbia. Some of these trees are 800 years old, and walking the trails through this virgin coastal forest can be quite an inspirational experience. Loop trails on either side of the highway lead awe-struck visitors through the mighty forest stands. The south loop showcases the largest Douglas-fir trees, with the biggest one measuring over 9 metres in circumference. The trail on the northern side of the road winds through groves of ancient Western Red Cedar to the shores of Cameron Lake. The 136-hectare park is located on Highway 4 on the shores of Cameron Lake, 11 miles (18 km) west of Errington.

Little Qualicum Falls Provincial Park straddles the scenic Little Qualicum River, where impressive waterfalls cascade and plummet down a rocky gorge in a beautiful forest setting. This magnificent 440-hectare park is a popular family recreation area, and is perhaps the most magnificent park on Vancouver Island, Little Qualicum Falls incorporates the entire southern shore of Cameron Lake, adjacent to MacMillan Provincial Park and the awesome Cathedral Grove Rainforest.

Cameron Lake: Spend an afternoon lazing on the beach at the Cameron Lake Recreation Site, surrounded by mountains and forests in the Little Qualicum Falls Provincial Park on Highway 4, 11 miles (18 km) west of Errington. Facilities at the lake include picnic sites, a boat Launch (private), and campsites (private and provincial). Cameron Lake is stocked with rainbow and cutthroat trout, and offers good fishing through summer. Anglers can test their fly fishing skills on the lake's brown trout, often the most difficult of trout to catch in B.C. Strong winds blow here in the afternoon, which attracts windsurfers but definitely deters those in small boats. Boaters and paddlers should take note of the strong and sudden gusts of wind often experienced on Cameron Lake.

At the west end of Cameron Lake is the Beaufort Picnic Site, another fine location for picnicking and swimming adjacent to the campground in the Little Qualicum Falls Provincial Park. Picnic tables are arranged beside the beach. Cameron Lake is bordered by steep mountains: Mt. Wesley to the north and Mt. Arrowsmith to the south.

The Kulth Music Fest is held in nearby Coombs in mid July. The Kulth is a festival created for people of all ages, with both local and international artists performing folk music, electronic music, and Reggae music. The festival is located at the Coombs Rodeo Grounds on the Alberni Highway.

Directly north of Errington is the seaside resort town of Parksville. Bordered by ocean and sheltered by mountains, Parksville boasts some of the finest beaches in Canada, including those at Rathtrevor Beach Provincial Park. When the tide goes out in Parksville, it leaves hundreds of metres of firm golden sand that is internationally acclaimed as the best building material for sandcastles!

To the northwest of Errington is Qualicum Beach, another Vancouver Island seaside pleasureland. Steeped in a quaint British heritage, modern day Qualicum Beach offers visitors the same gentle countryside and golden, seemingly endless sandy beaches as Parksville, plus 4 top golf courses.

Transportation

Travelling around Vancouver Island and the Gulf and Discovery Islands of British Columbia is a vacation in itself, whether by sea, land or air. We provide information on Air Services, BC Airports and Airlines, Bus and Coach operators, BC Ferries, Ferry Terminals and BC Ferry Routes, Taxis, Shuttles and Limousines, and the Rental of Boats, Cars, Trucks, Campers, RVs, Cycles, Scooters and Motorbikes.

Air : Air Services, Airports & Airlines

Find a commercial airline, air charter service, airport in British Columbia or any Canadian Province or territory, a scheduled flight, or that magical floatplane to drop you and your fishing gear off at a remote pristine lake in the wilderness of North Vancouver Island. Air services can get you to these fantasy destinations ... in a hurry.

Bus & Coach

Board luxury coaches for guided tours of local attractions, towns and countryside, beat the ferry lineup on a 'Vancouver to Victoria' scheduled bus service, or load your bike onto a suburban bus rack. You'll find an efficient, affordable network of public and private transport throughout the British Columbia islands.

Ferry : Terminals and Ferry Routes

Getting to Vancouver Island, the Gulf Islands, and the Sunshine Coast by BC Ferries and Washington State ferries is half the fun of travelling in the Pacific Northwest. BC Ferries serves up to 47 ports of call on 25 routes throughout coastal British Columbia. All mainland ferries feature vehicle, passenger and food services.

Boat Transport, Boat Rental & Water Taxis

Travel to remote and hard-to-reach places on the rugged Pacific Coast or the many straits and inland waters around Vancouver Island and the Gulf and Discovery Islands; Take a Water Taxi, charter a boat to transport your kayak and gear to the Broken Group or BC Gulf Islands, or rent a boat to cruise these spectacular waters.

Taxis, Shuttles & Limousines

Take advantage of the fast and friendly service around the towns and cities of BC, to the airports, or enjoy personalized pleasure tours travelling around Vancouver Island, courtesy of safe and professional drivers. The personal transport industry strives to achieve the highest standard of service and professionalism.

Rentals: Cars, Trucks & Motorhomes (RVs)

Set your own holiday schedule, your customized itinerary, and savour the freedom of exploring Vancouver Island at your own pace. Few places on earth are as suited to touring and exploring as Vancouver Island. Choose your own adventure amongst the lakes, rivers and mountains of this ruigged island, or simply rent a car to get about town.

Rentals: Bicycles, Scooters & Motorcycles

Tour the city streets and scenic country trails on a bicycle, or step it up a notch on a fun-to-ride scooter. If exhilaration is your thing, and you enjoy bugs in your teeth, then select from a range of touring motorcycles and head off into the rugged wilderness of Vancouver Island.

Ride Sharing

Need help to fill empty seats in your vehicle to increase vehicle occupancy and reduce costs? Want to travel all over the Pacific Northwest with friendly, verified drivers? Hitch hikers need to feel safe and comfortable when they're hitching a ride, and ride sharing can be safe and secure if done in an organized manner

Calendar of Events Vancouver Island

Farmers' Market - Tofino Public Market

Event Details
The Tofino Public Market Society presents Saturday markets between 10:00 AM and 2:00 PM on Tofino's Village Green Every Saturday from the May long-weekend to the end of September. "Make it, Bake it, Grow it, Gather it" is the market's principle. In a festive atmosphere with fresh food, live music and other activities, visitors and locals can shop and peruse from local artisans, home bakers, market gardeners, and wild food harvesters. Come down to the park and check out what people are making, baking, growing and gathering. May 20th to October 7th, 2017.

Queen of The Peak

Event Details
Queen of the Peak is an annual all women's surf championship, created by Surf Sister and Shelter Restaurant in 2010.

This fun, growing event showcases and celebrates the amazing female surf talent present here on the west coast – and beyond! Contest organizers focus efforts on designing the contest to be 'female-friendly' with free child care, dog-sitting services and even a massage tent that is complimentary for competitors.

Watch the Princess of the Peak competition, featuring gromettes as young as eight years old riding the waves.

Event Dates: Daily from September 29, 2017 to October 1, 2017

Event Location: Tofino Beaches, Tofino, BC

Hawk Watch (Drop-In Event) – All Ages

Vent Details
Queen of the Peak is an annual all women's surf championship, created by Surf Sister and Shelter Restaurant in 2010.

This fun, growing event showcases and celebrates the amazing female surf talent present here on the west coast – and beyond! Contest organizers focus efforts on designing the contest to be 'female-friendly' with free child care, dog-sitting services and even a massage tent that is complimentary for competitors.

Watch the Princess of the Peak competition, featuring gromettes as young as eight years old riding the waves.

Event Dates: Daily from September 29, 2017 to October 1, 2017

Event Location: Tofino Beaches, Tofino, BC

•

www.ingramcontent.com/pod-product-compliance
Lightning Source LLC
Chambersburg PA
CBHW021103080526
44587CB00010B/362